THE
UNSPEAKABLE

THE
UNSPEAKABLE

Denise Brown

DELAWARE

Newark: University of Delaware Press

Associated University Presses
2010 Eastpark Boulevard
Cranbury, NJ 08512

Portions of this book first appeared in slightly different form in *Northeast Magazine*.

The paper used in this publication meets the requirements of the American National Standard for Permanence of Paper for Printed Library Materials Z39.48-1984.

Library of Congress Cataloging-in-Publication Data

Brown, Denise, 1959-
    The unspeakable / Denise Brown.
        p. cm.
    ISBN-13: 978-0-87413-958-7 (alk. paper)
    ISBN-10: 0-87413-958-9 (alk. paper)
    1. Widows—United States—Psychology. 2. Loss (Psychology)
3. Widows—United States—Biography. 4. Brown, Denise, 1959-
I. Title.
HQ1058.5.U5B78 2006
155.9'37092—dc22
[B]
                                2006017256

For Ott

But now when I try to remember how it was, there is only a pit, and it's so dark, I cannot understand a thing.

—Czeslaw Milosz

Contents

Acknowledgments

Love and thanks to my parents, Jo and John Buel; my brother, Dr. Eric Buel, my gracious sister-in-law, Carol Harrington; and my children, Alex, Marion, and Elizabeth, my shining lights. To Peter Mlynarczyk, Mary Rubelmann, and Maggie Logan Jakubiak, for what we shared. To Patricia Jones, Dr. Marguerite Quintelli-Neary, Stephanie Hainsfurther, and Bill Williams, for patiently humoring along the writer and the writing all these years. To Dr. Donald Mender, for demystifying a variety of myths. To Lyn Bixby, Debbie Bixby, Dr. Patrick White, Dr. Jeanne Walker, Dr. Buck Beliles, and Susan Graham for gentle editorial advice and encouragement. To my agent, Ann Collette, and my attorney, Bill Gallagher, for expert assistance with the fine print. To Lary Bloom, Stephanie Summers, and Brian Toolan, for that first step, and Dick Boera, for the last. To Dr. Donald Mell for the green light, Drury Pifer for the blue pencil, and Dr. Charles Robinson for above and beyond, and especially for the *The*.

My children and I offer out sincere thanks to the people of the state of Connecticut, who opened their hearts to us when we were in need, and to the friends, neighbors, coaches, and teachers who helped us build a new life in the Northeast Kingdom of Vermont. We remain ever grateful.

Foreword

ON MARCH 6, 1998, A TROUBLED EMPLOYEE NEWLY RETURNED TO THE workplace after a long medical leave went on a rampage at the Newington headquarters of the Connecticut Lottery Corporation. He singled out four executives and killed them before turning the gun on himself. My husband, Otho R. Brown, president of the corporation, was among those murdered. He was fifty-four years old. We had been married nearly twelve years, and had three children.

In the weeks that followed, I began to keep a journal, jotting down my thoughts in a simple spiral-bound notebook at night when the house was quiet. In it, I recorded the tasks and occurrences of the difficult days, the evenings alone, the dreams that surfaced through fitful sleep. Quickly the journal became for me far more than a daybook of appointments to keep and things to do; I came to value it as something of a shelter in a maddening storm—a confessor of sorts, a steady, discreet companion to whom I could safely confide my concerns.

The Unspeakable is a memoir culled largely from the journals of that first year. It is as factually correct and forthright as those writings, my memory, and respect for the privacy of others will allow. It is a journey through grief, not an attempt to examine the crime itself, nor to lay blame on any doorstep. Its purpose is to contribute a countervoice to the love song of violence we so willingly sing in our society. To illustrate the devastation of a family with a father suddenly gone. To offer comfort to those who have suffered as well, to show how we survived.

Seven years have passed since my husband's death. From this vantage point, I have some trouble recognizing the woman who stumbles through these pages. She's me all right—there's no doubt—though I wonder if the ghost of a Sicilian great-grandmother, some injustice-righting *strega nona*, guided me then. With this memoir, she's had her say; she's laid bare the loss of that awful year. But that ghost—like others in my life and the specter of the woman I was—has found a certain measure of peace.

11

It's a beautiful life if you don't weaken, my mother-in-law, who lost her youngest son in his gorgeous youth and, thankfully, did not live to see the death of her beloved eldest, used to say. I recall her words often. I hope I can be forgiven my weaknesses. And I'm grateful for what feels like a largely un-deserved second chance to find that beauty once again.

Here in the rugged Northeast Kingdom of Vermont, in this new world, I write and cook, and occasionally teach. I throw dinner parties, research the next novel, record my days and dreams in simple journals. In good weather, I garden; last summer, I had remarkable success with parsley, and with peach-colored roses. My children are healthy and strong-willed, curious and non-chalant, and about as content as sibling teenagers corralled together are likely to be.

Death has been cheated. He no longer rides at my elbow.

August 2005

THE
UNSPEAKABLE

1

March 6

I LEARN OF IT ON THE TELEVISION. I'VE BEEN SITTING AT THE COMPUTER, answering e-mail, conferring on an esoteric literary project I am soon to abandon, the biography of a beautiful, twisted woman whose life for me in a matter of moments will cease to have meaning. I stop for coffee and a bite to eat. I carry in a mug and toast, and switch on the set in the den.

There she is, the early-morning news anchor, speaking into the microphone she holds in her steady hand, the gray stone of a parking lot behind her. There's been a shooting, she says, and names the location, her voice inconceivably calm, it's what they pay her for, that voice, that control, the steel in her eye, that on-air command. Several people have been wounded, she continues. At least one confirmed dead.

I know the location. I know the parking lot. I know that one dead is my husband, and I start to scream.

I just know.

I grab the phone, forgetting the number, trying to reach anyone at the corporation. It rings and rings; there's no one there to answer. I can't breathe. It's insane, unreal, the news on the television, it can't be true. I call my good friend who lives nearby, she comes over immediately, her hair still wet from the shower, her eyes wide, frightened. She sits beside me, rubbing my arm, and we watch the screen, but there's nothing, no more news, just the blonde with her microphone, repeating what she is allowed to report, shots of the building, ambulances, police cars. My friend calls 911.

People start to arrive. The tall, calm chief of police. An officer who parks in my driveway and patrols the door, stands guard outside when there's need. A neighbor who's just heard, then another, and another still. They hug me, then step aside, mill about nearby or take seats in silence, not knowing what to say. One sits at the dining-room table, phone in hand, authoritatively making call after call, calls to the hospital in Hartford, calls to those who know but can tell us officially nothing, and it's too much. I stand at the kitchen sink, staring out the window, numb and shaking.

They've taken the employees away from the scene in buses, taken them to a safe civic building where they are questioned, comforted, given access to telephones. But Ott doesn't call. No one calls. Not his assistant, not his vice president, nobody, and I'm angry that those who know what has happened will tell me nothing.

Maybe no news is good news, someone says, or I say to myself, and go into the bathroom and splash my face with water, brush my hair. He might walk in the door any second—would I want him to see me looking like this? Any second now he'll come home, and this horrid morning will be shown up for what it is, a bad dream, a close call.

But I know it won't be so. Everyone knows. I never ask to be driven to the corporation, or to that safe civic building. No one suggests it either, no one wants to make that trip. Everyone knows how this will end.

Two hours pass this way, in waiting and not waiting, in trance, in tears shed while standing against the wall, unable to move, or sitting stone mute at the kitchen table. "You better call your folks, call his sister," the police chief tells me, even though he can't get anyone to confirm the facts. He's made a half-dozen calls of his own; still, no one will verify our worst fear. "Better let them know before they hear it on the news."

And, indeed, before I know for sure, before the uniformed trooper and the corporate suits arrive to officially inform the family, reporters are on the phone, calling for comment, calling from Boston, from God knows where. My friend answers the phone, hangs up in disgust. A man with a video camera stands at the foot of my driveway, as close to the property as the police will allow, filming my children as a neighbor brings them home from school. By early afternoon, there are reporters at the scene from every channel, relating the news that the gunman and four others are now confirmed dead, playing over and over footage of sobbing survivors, of the governor arriving somber and strong, of ambulances, and of heavily laden gurneys being set inside them. Of a handful of detectives examining my husband's body lying half-covered in the gravel parking lot.

The following morning the newspaper will use that image, blurred and shadowed, shot from a respectful distance through a telephoto lens. They'll make a poster out of it for their front page.

So you see, then, how the nightmare begins. This is how it begins. Maybe you've envisioned it yourself, it's not so difficult to imagine, it could be your own husband you've kissed and watched drive off to work on a Friday morning. Your own husband, your love, your truest friend chased across a parking lot an hour later, losing a shoe and stumbling, shot once and falling hard, then the man with the gun running toward him, reaching him at last, standing over him, for how long? An eternity, a snap of the fingers, how long? It takes maybe three seconds to reload a gun, the handsome sergeant will tell me some weeks later. What are three seconds of begging for your life to be spared, lying on a bed of stone in your own blood, a killer methodically reloading, then leveling the barrel at your head? How long must those three seconds have been, I cannot help but ask myself.

The last words he heard on this earth were, *Fuck you.*
I am amazed I have not gone out of my mind.

He needs clothes, our quiet neighbor whispers to me that afternoon, and I choose favorites, a golf shirt and slacks, and then hours later, after he's worked on, prepared, cleaned up, they take me to see him. It's dark, already late on the longest day of my life, that first Friday in March.

He's lying on a draped table, too unnatural to be sleeping, his body straight and still, his hands clenched upon his abdomen. I reach for them and shudder to find them so very cold, immovable, I'm not prepared, not at all. Of course, I think, yes, he would be cold, it's to be expected, but grief whips through me. Our closest neighbors sit nearby and wait, an hour, maybe more. I touch him, kiss him, caress him, it's too much, too much to bear, too much to watch, and my friend says, her voice low and kind, *it's not him, it's only his shell, he's not there,* but I can't pull away. His face is locked in a grimace, his eyes are shut tight, his mouth is a bitter line. And the temple, the right temple, it's patched, it has the feel of soft plastic, a good job I'm sure, I touch the wound, I kiss the wound, I rub my hands on his shoulders, to warm them, maybe I can warm the flesh. I embrace him as best I can. And at one point I hear myself shout, *I want some of his hair!* I turn back, try to catch the eye of the woman in the dark suit, the funeral director. *Don't forget! I want a lock of his hair!* And our good neighbor says, *Oh, Denise, are you sure?*

They leave me alone, and I kiss him everywhere, from the top of his head to his toes, from the fingers of one hand to the fingers of the other, a game we played, not often enough. Our *I love you* in kisses, from here to there, everywhere, one last time, and I stop, return to his hands—stubborn as carved stone, too fixed to twine, one into another, with my own.

To hold those hands once more.

Do you know that sound, the sound of pure grief that erupts from the core of your being, from your heart and lungs and gut, and fills you, empties you of everything else, of every other thought or hope or prayer? It is savage, wordless, that sound. It is like the howl of an animal dying alone in a black forest. An animal poisoned or half-eaten, caught in the steel teeth of a trap, its flesh ripped and spirit broken, with nothing but the certainty of death for comfort.

I have heard that sound filling a darkened room around me, felt it consuming my body, unloading my soul of everything I once believed. I cannot recognize the woman from whom the sound emerges. She's barely human, she barely exists. She ought to be put down like an old horse, put out of her misery once and for all. Somebody should get a gun.

Finally, sleep falls and quiets that sound. Blessed sleep, and with it simple blackness, or flashes of dream, not all of them terror-filled. In the morning, the sun does rise. Children emerge hungry from their beds. House cats meow and demand attention. Crocuses defy all odds and bloom along the garden walkway. A few notes of a love song float through the open window of a passing car.

The woman I don't recognize gets out of bed. She cannot lie there and die. That choice, longed for as it might be, is too easy, too selfish. She is no longer a wife, but she is a mother. She is a mother of children who need her pulled together, on her feet, standing strong as she can in the face of the unthinkable. That woman I cannot name gets out of bed, and she gets on with things.

In the darkness, then, under the cover of night, I cry, I let the grief pour out of me. The images overwhelm me, I lie down with them, I swallow them whole. Sometimes I dream. When I do, my dreams are angry, my anger rages against my father, who is God, who is Ott, who was the world as I knew it and now no longer exists.

By day, I avoid what I can. I let the phone ring, I hide when a good neighbor comes to the door. I keep away from windows. The simplest chores deplete me. I make lists of the tasks that cannot be escaped, cross out the items, one by one:

Social Security forms.

Must send for certified copy of marriage license, death certificates.

Fax the will to his sister.

Accountant. Taxes.

Thank-you notes.

The names of recommended therapists.

Conversations revolve around finances. Incredible. My husband is dead, he's been killed, he's been chased down and shot dead by a man who stood over him with a gun while he lay on the ground, suffering, yet we sit at the kitchen table talking about money. And then I even dream about money, about paperwork, about more and more forms piling up, filling a room. Why must I deal with this now? I lash out at people who are only trying to help me. I fix my anger on the smallness of their concerns, the pettiness, because I am powerless to quiet what lies at the heart of my grief. I pray. I pray I will be forgiven, understood. I am not myself.

He is not on a business trip.
He is never coming home.
It's like a line from a movie, or out of a paperback novel. "When my husband was shot and killed . . ." "After my husband was murdered, I . . ."
I did what?

I can't cook, I can't eat. I feed the kids the junk-food meals of their dreams. We pretend we are just having a little snack, sitting on the living-room floor, watching television. Sometimes I even spread a blanket, as if for a picnic. Mostly I take them out, by day, by night. They order whatever they like. I hand the waitress my credit card, avoiding her eyes.

One day at lunch I notice other women. They are dressed in fine suits or lovely spring sweaters and skirts, their hair recently cut, their nails brightly polished. They smile at the men who sit across from them, flirt with them, bring a free, jeweled hand to their hair in a hint of suggestion, tilt their heads ever so slightly to one side. Some of the men are husbands; some are not their own. It's not so hard to tell who belongs to whom, who simply desires. But everyone I see seems uniquely attractive, universally light in spirit.

One older woman, her gray hair twisted into a strange cone at the top of her head, eats her salad and soup alone, only a book for company.

He died without me. He died a miserable death, and I wasn't there.
My duty as his wife—my privilege, to be by his side—was stolen from me.

The women call, they call and call, they want to come over, they want to bring me and the kids home-cooked meals and the comfort they feel their presence will afford. The men come too, handing bags of warm bagels or bottles of Chianti through the half-opened door, then hurrying away.

I drink the wine. I drink it right away. The food, someone else will consume.

The morning of the funeral the house fills with people, people standing about in uncomfortable clothing with drained expressions and nothing to say. I can't tolerate it a moment more, and retreat to the bedroom and then the bath, where I fix my hair and make up again, again. It's hopeless, but I try. The face shows everything and nothing. It is vacant and horrifying. It is appalling to have to call it my own.

There are no tears this morning, the tears have poured out of me; there is only a gripping ache in my stomach, the hallucinatory dance and pace of a dream. I look at my watch, it's nearly time to go. *Where is Ott?* I say to myself, examining the band and the simple oval face as if they were made of rubies and pure gold, all logic and reasoning lost to me. *Where is he? We have to leave for the church soon. We'll be late.*

I've allowed the reporters into the balcony. I want them to photograph the governor. I want that for my children. I know the power of an image and I want that for them, the governor speaking at their father's funeral, I already know the words he will say, I've written them in my mind. The priest tells me they cannot photograph anyone in the pews, only those who step to the altar. It never occurs to me that they will photograph my family as we file in. A grim shot for the next day's front page, me with my head sunk low, escorted like an invalid, a helper at my elbow, my daughters skittish in flowered dresses, my son without expression, my parents drawn and dark.

Five or six hundred fill the church. Employees of the corporation bused in. Parishioners and neighbors I barely know or have never met. Government officials. Colleagues of Ott from all over the country, from across the Atlantic. The priest speaks movingly, guiding my son and daughters to remember their father's love, making a comparison between the sacrifice of Christ and that of my husband, one that will elicit a few well-meaning jokes after the day is done. The children wear their sadness and confusion like stone masks on their beautiful faces. They find it impossible to sit still. By turns the girls ask to perch on my lap. Men from the corporation rise disheartened but resolved, they talk about him, they reminisce, they praise, they console. I hear and I don't hear. I look about, look at the faces filling the pews, see them staring back at me. Nothing is real. My mind travels elsewhere, anywhere but this church, this service, this day. I simply breathe and get through it.

The governor steps thoughtfully to the podium and addresses the mourners. His voice is clear, sorrowful but assured. He does not disappoint me. He knows exactly what I want my children to hear, the words they will repeat again and again to their friends, to each other, in the weeks that follow. The entire funeral and all the preparation, the reading and the song decisions, the hiring of the limousine, the exotic flowers for the altar, the catered coffee and sandwiches, the endless line of greeting after the service—it is all for this, this brief moment, these few words. The governor of the state of Connecticut, commanding and polished in his elegant attire, standing in the house of God, calling my husband a hero.

This is what happened that Friday morning in March. Simply then, I will tell you. The simple facts as best I can say them.

There was a man with a gun and knife and a long-seated grudge. He'd come prepared to kill each day that week, and on Friday he carried it out. He killed three fine, irreplaceable people inside the mazelike walls of the corporation's headquarters. He intended to kill more. My husband was the president, he was on the man's list. He told the employees to run, out of the building, into the safety of the woods, and then he stayed in sight, in the gravel parking lot, where the man would easily find him, where he'd not harm anyone else.

I'm sure he thought he could run. Yes, he would have believed that. For Ott, nothing was impossible.

The man in charge of security ran into the woods, too. From the woods, he watched my husband fall, he watched the man reload his gun. He stopped running and watched. I don't know if he watched while the man executed my husband, or if at that point he turned his face away. Others saw, though. Others called out for the man with the gun standing over my husband to stop. They screamed out his name, yelled at him, attracted attention, put themselves in danger as well. But not the man in the woods. He turned his face and ran half a mile, he ran far and fast, he ran away from it all.

This, then, is the image that remains for me, that flashes against the cold black canvas of my mind by day and night. An image not of the Governor, not even of the man with the gun. The man with the gun does not exist, he's evaporated into the darkness of his own soul, he's nothing more than bad air rising off a dying sea. It is only Ott who remains. Only the vision of him in the parking lot holds on. Those final moments, those three seconds, the last plea, the filthy curse. My husband's arm rising up before his eyes. His blood seeping into a berth of stone.

This is the image I cannot escape. There is no safe wood for me to hide in, nowhere for me to run, no direction in which to turn my face away.

2

Lost

I SPOKE AT HIS FUNERAL, TOO. I HAD TO SPEAK, I HAD TO SAY A FEW WORDS, unremarkable except for what happened while they were being written. Two nights before the service, we sit at the kitchen table, Ott's sister with the newspaper, turning pages, reading them or not. I'm across from her with a pen and yellow pad. It's evening, the wall of glass doors behind us is cold and black, the house finally quiet. While I'm thinking, writing, the lamp in the hallway explodes. There's a bang, a flash of light into the darkened foyer, the air becomes charged, fills with bitter ozone. Later, when we check, we see burn marks around the base, gray flares on the white ceiling. Days later, when it's repaired, we learn how lucky we are that it had not caused a fire.

We look up from our blurred pages, look up at each other, my sister-in-law and I, the sharp clap still in our ears and that smell in the air, and we know, we are certain, we are without doubt. It's a sign. It's Ott.

I cling to this. I cling to that hope that something of him survives. It's a lunacy, maybe, or a solemn truth revealed. I don't care which. I hold on to it tight.

Only later, much later, will I make the connection between the words I'd written and the explosion in the hall. Those words, scrawled at the top of the page, the very top, the words with which my eulogy would begin. "Ott was the bright light in my life."

It's too coincidental, from the distance of years. Something a lazy director might add to spice up a dull movie plot, an unsubtle slap no cinema viewer would miss. Yet then I did, too numb to notice. Though now, sometimes, I let the synchronicity cheer me.

Look for coincidences, my cousin says, the cousin who believes we are all light, all energy, all travelers spending a short time on this school we call

22

earth before journeying on to a brighter place. *Look for coincidences, because there aren't any.*

The news media continue their coverage, their barrage of words and images. The weekend cleanup of blood and gore inside the corporation, the well-attended funerals, and the opinions of cautious legislators and self-appointed experts on violence in the workplace fill the front sections of newspapers, dominate the television stations' first five minutes of broadcast news. They replay the same footage over and over, repeat the same arguments in the editorial pages.

Murder sells. Any scrap of quote, any morbid detail or solemn scene—a draped casket carried from the church, a flower set reverently on bloodied stone—is worthy of ink or film.

The father and mother of the man with the gun are newsworthy, too, of course. They have something to say and they do. They write an apology. They send a copy not to each of the victims' families, but to the newspaper. It's short, just a few paragraphs, but I read it without comprehension, floating my eyes over the text, it makes little impression on me, nothing of it touches, nothing of it moves. Later I recall only that they want the world to know their son was not a monster. What he did was monstrous, they say, but he was not a monster.

I don't know what to think of this, of their words, their apology. It's absurd. What must a man do, then, how many must he kill before I am allowed to use the word "monster"? No, I can't think of the parents' sorrowful letter, their brief postscript to mass murder. It's not addressed to me, anyway. It's addressed to the world at large. I cannot think about it, I cannot understand it at all.

Because, you see, I know about the sign on their door. I've read of it in the same newspaper. The sign posted on the front door of their home, the gunman's boyhood home, the one to which he's returned, too sick to live on his own. The father has stuck the sign there, it's his door, his sign. And when it's reported in the newspaper, he will say it's only a joke. It's a joke. This, then, is the joke, the sign on the door. This is what it reads:

Trespassers will be shot.
Survivors will be shot again.

For a long while, a very long while, I want the father of the man with the gun shot, too. I want him shot dead. He has trespassed grievously into my life, and I want the judgment he has deemed fair meted out. I want him chased across a parking lot and shot while he suffers. I want him to suffer.

It will be a very long while indeed before I begin to understand that he and his wife suffer, to feel a semblance of compassion for them, to begin some process of simple understanding. Not forgiveness. I do not comprehend forgiveness, it is a concept beyond my shattered reality, it is a word that has lost all meaning. The world itself and my role in it have lost all meaning, my relationship to other people, to the place I live and walk and breathe, to possessions I've carted about from house to house, all now cast in a confusing, mortifying light. But after a long stretch of time, there comes something resembling the birth of understanding, or perhaps acceptance, something another person might call the beginning of healing, in the slowest, most painful steps, in simple decisions. To bring a pot of salted water to a boil for pasta, to wear a lovely silk blouse the color of the sea, to say in time a prayer for the parents of the man with the gun. To not live entirely in those moments in the parking lot. To rise up from the bed of gray stone.

I will write those lines, *Trespassers will be shot. Survivors will be shot again*, in my journal, here and there, apropos of nothing and everything. I will write them over and over, each time trying to believe that a human being, someone made of flesh and blood, someone presumably with a soul, could post such a thing on the door of his own home.

I fantasize about meeting the father. I want to meet him, I want to look into his eyes, I want to see beyond the glassy blankness I imagine I'll find into whatever is there, darkness or light or nothing at all. I want to meet the man who would keep an arsenal of guns in his home, knowing his son is ill, knowing he's tried to kill himself several times. This then is the only thing I will say to him, in the clearest, most dispassionate voice I can muster: *Trespassers will be shot*, I'll recite, my head held high and still. *Survivors will be shot again*. He will know then, he will see in my own eyes, what the evil he has spawned has rendered.

The flowers are dying. All over the house, the once lovely arrangements, the death baskets and bouquets, the fulsome sprays and centerpieces are wilting, turning brown and ragged, dropping shriveled leaves and petals. The perfume of decaying flowers is overwhelming, like the stench off a dark river.

The priest arrives promptly at two for our talk. I have invited him. I welcome this visitor. It is a few days after the funeral. We step into the sunroom, sit at a glass-topped table. Someone has watered these living plants, the clay pots of overgrown geraniums and African violets, the hanging baskets of flowering ivy and impatiens. In this bright room, the smell of damp earth fills the warm air pleasantly. I set out a plate of fruit and nut bread slices, small bowls of butter and cream cheese to spread on them, mugs of hot coffee. The priest eats as if he has an appetite, as if the gesture pleases him. His glasses reflect strong squares of sunlight. His hair is neatly combed, recently trimmed.

I can't find any words. My own Bible is at my left hand, and I run my fingers across the cover. I can't bring myself to talk of the sadness, can't share the grief with him, only my anger, and that only on the most superficial level, practically intellectual. I thank him for his good work. I press the need to pursue the truth, to know the facts about my husband's death. I tell him I expect to return to the church. Only briefly do I speak of the nightmares, my worries for the children, how much I miss Ott, how awful and unending the evenings are alone.

I hear myself say, toward the end of the priest's visit, as the refilled mugs empty again, that I am angry at the universe. I am angry at God.

Some nights later, after piling the stems and blossoms into a huge plastic bag and asking my son to dump it well into the woods behind the house, I dream of all those flowers rotting in room after room. I dream of more arriving each day, of a young man delivering an armful of violet tulips and with them, a long, white, ribbon-tied box. He hands that box to me graciously, and I open it, expecting roses, and find instead my husband's severed right hand.

I will never thank everyone who has sent flowers. I write a few notes, my eyes tearing, my handwriting failing me, ripping up sheet after sheet of ruined stationery and starting again. Then I cannot bear the task at all. I bundle up the cards, drop them into an envelope and hide them away. It will be nearly two years before I can stand to look at them again.

I call the acting president at home, the man who has taken over for my husband at the corporation. He's not in. His wife talks to me, tries to comfort me, as she will many times over the months to come. I want to know what she knows about the psychiatrist, where he lives, where he practices, why he let the man with the gun come back to work.

She tells me no one knows anything about him. No one's been in contact with him, no one can reach him. "It's like he dropped off the face of the earth."

Maybe so, but I know his name. It's in the newspapers, a common name, a name you might find on a mailbox on any street in America. I look in the phone book for his number, but I cannot say why I don't call. Maybe I'm not sure I've found the right man in the jumble of listings. Maybe I know I'll regret it, whatever I say to him, whatever spews out from my grief, a tirade of hate, a swell of incomprehensible sobs. For some time, I kneel by the bed, shaking, the book in my hands, the phone at the ready. I don't call.

So I've never spoken a word to him. Not a word.

I take up drinking. I take it up, I make a conscious decision, one of the few I bother to make and then attempt to keep. I take up drinking with the enthusiasm of embracing a delightful hobby, like hand-stitching fine linens or soldering stained-glass panels into colorful lamps. I practice faithfully until I have the method down cold; I lay in supplies for the long haul. I drink like the proverbial fish.

It is not, I suppose, a therapy highly recommended by priests or psychiatrists, but it damn sure works for me. I drink so I can't feel, can't think, can't clearly envision those last three seconds. I drink to avoid the world I no longer wish to be part of. I drink simply to get through the day. Drink becomes my reliable friend, my unfailing sympathizer, my ready helpmate, always close at hand. I get to know alcohol, to crave it, to welcome the burn of whiskey at the back of my throat, the subtle lull of deep-red wines, the medicinal effect of gin without tonic. I know it as I used to know the satisfactions of a simple tomato sauce over a bowl of linguini or a glass of sweet iced tea on a hot afternoon. Drink becomes for me food, water, sleep.

For the better part of six months, I stay more or less soused.

One evening, well into a bottle of something red, the mother of a friend of my girls calls. She's kind, she's concerned, she wants to tell me about the Lord God.

It's late, it's nine-thirty or better. It's more than I can bear, this conversation. I already have a good idea about the Lord God, and quite frankly, He's not the man I thought He was. I try to listen as the woman tells me her multilayered religious history, how she's come to know the Truth. She's talking to me about Free Will, how the man with the gun exercised Free Will to murder four people and then himself, and somehow, this is all in the workings of the benevolent universe created out of nothing by the Lord God himself. "The Lord God loves us and cares for us," she says.

I agree. What's not to agree?

"The Lord God loves us and cares for us, but He lets us make our own decisions," the woman explains. "He loves us and cares for us, but he doesn't intervene in our lives."

I ponder this. In some other time and place, in conversation exchanged in a graceless rectory basement, over sweetened coffee after a sedate Sunday morning sermon, perhaps this all might make sense. But just now it does not.

"If the Lord God loves us and cares for us," I ask, "but doesn't intervene in our lives, then what the hell good is He?"

I don't remember when they come, the men and the woman from the corporation, the somber suits, my husband's friends and colleagues, but they do, not long after he's been killed. They come to my house with papers in their hands, with an extra copy for me, they come with little to say but a careful recitation of what's printed on the sheets before them. The corporate attorney comes, too, a young man with a family; I've met his wife, I like her. I like them both without reservation.

I like and respect the others, too. It won't last.

We are already adversaries, these men, this woman, these survivors of the siege. How could I not have known it? Their bodies, their faces, the very papers they hold, should have told me the lines had already been drawn, the lines behind which we will take our stands, the shifting line in the sand between right and wrong we will never agree upon.

I should have known.

They read from the papers and tell me of workman's compensation benefits, of a fund they will set up to facilitate a gift from a vendor, of education trusts for the kids. It all sounds good, doesn't it?—the recitation of what's printed on the papers before them, the list of the things they tell me they will do, to help me, to ease me through this. What more could I want? What more could any woman possibly want or expect or need? It's all written there on those two sheets, my rights under law to appropriate compensation, the selected benefits to which I am entitled.

The truth about what led to my husband's murder doesn't happen to be one of them.

There is nothing more sacred and unknowable in this society, no secret more closely guarded, than the high-level, liability-culpable, bureaucratic fuck-up.

I am sitting on the overstuffed sofa in our game room. He's been dead only a few days, a week at most. There are flowers everywhere still, baskets and vases of pink and yellow and white blooms on low tables around me, beginning to fade and collapse. Someone is talking to me, someone is trying to talk some sense into me. "You need an attorney," she says, this neighbor and friend of mine. "You have to see an attorney." It has to be done, it's the only way. She has names, she knows the best in the state. Her husband will make the contact for me.

Oh, no, I say to her. *No, no, no.* Ott wouldn't want that, wouldn't want me to follow that route. He built the corporation, he gave his life to it, they will do the right thing. They will tell the truth about what happened, they will tell the truth about what was done, what was left undone, why four innocent people are now dead. They will see it through now to the necessary end, they will ask the questions in my heart, they won't let his death be in vain.

I tell her this, I say this out loud. I believe it with all my heart. I truly believe.

My friend's husband is an attorney himself. She's kind, she's careful, she doesn't judge me, doesn't say outright how utterly foolish and naive I am, how thoroughly wrong I will be proven, but she presses, she guides. Part of me must know she is right, because I hear her. I send the fax, I let her husband make the appointment. Part of me must recognize there is no choice.

Some weeks later, they take me to him, I meet the man who will represent me in this horror, the one who may find a "remedy," as my friend's husband says. A remedy for mass murder. It's preposterous, but that's the term, what you might call a quick fix for a bad cough, a thick red syrup in a bottle spooned out to a sick child, or a tonic, something hawked for a few dollars at a carnival.

He doesn't rise to greet us, doesn't greet us at all, as much as I can remember. He's somber and businesslike, reviewing the papers I've brought, his arms sheathed in a crisp white shirt, the cuffs embellished with touches of gold. He's a busy man, he's highly respected, he's the best there is. I'm lucky, I'm told, that he's taken the time to even see me.

I don't feel lucky.

I sit across the table from him in a cluttered workroom facing the street, cardboard boxes tossed and stacked about, shelves of law books reaching to the high Victorian ceiling. The anger seethes inside me; surely anyone within the range of my aura must feel it, the very blackness of it, the utter stink of rage. I want heads on platters. I want people to pay. The vision of my husband's death never leaves my mind.

I sign a paper, signing over a third of any judgment that might be recovered, signing over my life, I think. One third of the remedy—yes, let's find a remedy. And then with that done, my friends take me out to lunch. It's almost a celebration, as if today significant movement in the direction one must somehow crawl toward has been made. I order red wine, and after a few sips the shaking in my arms and legs subsides.

Years later, I am still grieving over the appalling litigation, having my signature notarized on hideous documents, lamenting everything connected with Connecticut, with lawyers, with the corporation. Years later I am sure there is no such thing as justice in this world. I know nothing the lawyer can do will bring him back, nothing will make anyone tell the truth or show remorse, nothing will remotely prove a remedy, and I wonder if I ought not move beyond the desire for these things, move beyond fury, move beyond my very life itself.

That March I learn to make lists, a comforting habit, my lists of things to do to anchor my sanity. One day I make a list of thirteen death-related chores.

I dream again and again of giving birth to infants who never take a breath, of a plane crash and the suffocating fire that follows, of Ott lying on the bed of stone and me beside him, not yet dead, the man with the gun standing above me, pointing the gray barrel at my temple.

And I dream many nights of driving long distances over unfamiliar terrain, of driving in ruined cities, in violent weather, in blinding rain and pelting ice. I dream of fleeing horrific collisions in a crushing onslaught of traffic. I drive on and on, wanting to be anywhere other than where I am, anywhere at all. I long to escape.

When I'm awake I dream of it, too, of that cherished escape, of running to the car and slipping into the snug front seat, swerving out of the drive, the sun lowering, the sky turning milky white in the final gasp of day. I see myself race along the wooded road just beyond our affluent town, taking the winding shortcut from one busy drag to another, along the grounds of the exclusive boarding school that reminds me of a medieval castle, on toward the cold, muddy fields where our children play soccer.

I'll let the accelerator race, embrace those roads like the madwoman I have become, shadows deepening, sky darkening, my fingers playing lightly on the wheel, my very breath fueling the engine. And on that sharp curve just beyond the short straightaway, the palm of my hand will twist quick and precise, as if in a gesture of an ancient dance, the sensual movement of a woman a sculptor might render in bronze. In that quick, sure flex of an upturned wrist, I'll send my soul headlong and high before me, and with the perfect aim of the truly deranged, sail the car straight into the trunk of a sturdy oak.

Trespassers will be shot.
Survivors will be shot again.

The psychiatrist has a soothing voice. Over the phone we set up an appointment. He knows who I am. Everyone knows. I am the widow down the street. I am the woman whose husband died suffering in the parking lot. I am easy to define.

I imagine the shrink, picture him younger than he turns out to be, craft a vision of medical knighthood, a savior on a white horse. His office is a tiny, crowded affair at the end of a narrow hall. His features are sharp, his eyes guarded behind glasses. He is dressed in neutrals, cool colors, like wet and dry sand, as if brighter tones might upset me, might spook me like a ruffling flag in the wind, as if I were a flighty horse crossing a rickety bridge. He sits back and observes me, his long legs stretched and crossed. He rarely interjects. He wants me to talk without direction. He nods, he encourages, tells me that we have much work to do, and lets me find it. Now and then he jots down notes on a small spiral-bound pad, as I jump from topic to topic. I tell him of my nightmares, of my paranoid mistrusts and fears. I offer my own analysis of the dream of my husband's severed hand.

And I wear bright pink lipstick to see him. I don't know why. As if my appearance is not ridiculous enough, exhaustion contorting my face, weighing down my shoulders. The hour goes by, much of it in tears. I don't want to be here. I'm not ready for this. I'm not ready for analysis or counseling or whatever term this therapy demands. It's too much, too early, too organized, too hopeful. I'll come once more, maybe twice, to see the white knight who has been so highly recommended. I'll go through the motions, take a few of the pills he prescribes to help me sleep, a few of the others to calm me during the day. But soon I cancel appointments and console myself with gin.

The children have a shrink, too, a postdoctoral student from Yale, sent to us through a state agency. He talks to me first, sits with me in my warm sunroom filled with the plants I have not yet parched to death. He's depressingly young, of course, tall and dark, reserved and modest; he seems to have no idea how entirely attractive he is. I feel simply ancient sitting near him.

Then he talks to the kids, asks them indirect questions, visits their rooms, takes part in their game of pool. His visit annoys them, though they feign a childish gratitude, unfurl a singular politeness for the adult who perhaps has come to judge them, or more likely, judge their mother's care. But they're bored with him, bored with the business end of death, they don't want to talk of sad things or be scrutinized by a stranger. "Does he have to come again?" they ask when he leaves.

I think, later in their lives, they may seek out a man just like him and try to unravel the dark horror of their childhood. I think, from time to time, even in these early weeks, we have wrapped the wound all too clean and tight.

One morning I wake up and he has been dead a whole month.
One morning it is my birthday, and I don't realize it until the afternoon.

In odd moments something comes over me—nothing short of delusion, a brief insanity, a frantic trance. I think I should sell the house right away and move to Italy, where no one will know us. Live on a rocky, barren island where we'll swim all day at the shore's edge beneath the lemon yellow Mediterranean sun, where I'll learn to tie fishing nets and toss them into the water and raise a bounty from the sea. The air rushes into my lungs and I'm alive, I'm delirious with life itself, the precious, awful absurdity of it, and I want to belt out old songs I know by heart, paint huge canvases with blooming flowers in ruby, topaz, the truest greens. I want to open a restaurant, race a team of sled dogs across the snow, spend a weekend in a far city with a Russian lover. I want to forget myself, I want to exist. I want every crazy thing I've ever wanted in my life, all at once, all in one breath.

But more than anything, I want my husband back. I want him alive. And in my madness, in my moments of utter possession, I believe in resurrection, in Lazarus, in miracles. God help me, I believe that if I dream and wish and pray, if I cast my life as a sorcerer's spell, charge the atmosphere, command the elements, prepare a meal for him worthy of a king, Ott will rise out of the blackness and come home. I believe, I know in my heart, if only I had faith like a grain of mustard seed, it could come to be. It's my fault he's not here, it's my fault he's still gone; if only I were strong enough, resourceful, spiritual, whole, I could reach down into what's left of my soul and find the precise sum to pay his ransom. I could build the bridge between life and death out of the air itself. I could bring him back.

Where is he? a good friend asks, gently, her voice not betraying her Buddhist disbelief, when I tell her I still feel him, that part of him survives, that he's simply not dead. *Where do you send your thoughts?*

I can't put it into words. It's not a place, not the way our limited senses conceive of place, of being and time, in our minds. It's everywhere and nowhere, I think. Another dimension and reality, some world that meets our own on a strange and distant horizon.

I just say, *I see him in dreams. I ask him to come to me in my dreams, and sometimes he does.*

I want to climb to the top of a tall mountain, steep and spectacular, ice-capped against a turquoise blue sky. I want to climb high, spread my arms wide and drink in the cold air, and then scream out, to whoever will listen, whoever might hear, *Teach love. Teach love.*

And in the whispering echo that follows, in the chorus left in the wind, I'll lean forward and let my body fall straight down into the darkness below.

I buy a new skillet, and hanging baskets of impatiens for the front porch, and two gallons of paint the color of Pepto-Bismol. I paint the living room this color. I work late into the night, the kids asleep, the floor covered with old sheets. It's an appalling shade, not far from putrid, even worse in daylight, and I know it, but I don't care. It's pink, it's bright, it's different, and that's all that matters, that something is different, something is not beyond my control, even if it is merely the shocking pink on the walls.

In the process, our friendly mongrel ends up pink. She wiggles about in her happy dance, little splotches of pink stamped on her black tail, rump, nose. I find this surreally hilarious.

It's not quite so easy to be heartbroken in a bright pink room, I tell myself, as I busy my hands and mind.

Where are the children during this time, their father dead, their mother quickly deteriorating? They are there, of course, with me, my blood, my being, little phantoms of what they were just weeks before, disembodied voices behind closed doors, vulnerable strangers passing in the halls. They wade through their tedious days in school, waiting for weekends when other women will invite them over to be with their friends, to eat real meals with salads and cooked meats and bread and butter, to sleep in beds with freshly laundered sheets. They crave normalcy, even if it's borrowed. They know nothing will ever be normal in our home again.

My neighbors rally. They gather up the kids for pizza, they cart them to soccer and lacrosse games, they help me throw birthday parties. They set up a scholarship fund for their education, a fund that will raise thousands of dollars. I don't deserve it, I think, all this support, I barely know these folks. We've lived in this town a short two years, a blink of an eye in the isolation of affluent suburbia.

I don't know if I appreciate it all, just then. I don't know if I realize how much I have to be grateful for. Some days it is all I can do to get out of bed and keep my feet under me.

Even with this help, one day it is too much for us. We are zombies, numb and blind and indifferently bitter; we are at each other's throats. I keep the kids out of school, and we head for an amusement park. It's a depressing little place, it seems to me, with feeble rides and expensive, antiquated games, but it's a change and we need it. I've brought a wallet full of twenty-dollar bills, and one by one they go. It doesn't matter. The kids are smiling, they're acting goofy and running around like puppies, they're exchanging their winning tickets for silly trinkets. I sit nibbling pizza, watching them trot from game to game. Young mothers with preschool children look at me oddly. They must think me a fugitive, fleeing with my brood, on the run from the law or abuse or both. I can't help but recall when my own children were so small and carefree, what it was like to hold a tiny child, to love with no need for words or worry beyond food and sleep and breath.

I tell myself I should adopt a baby, somehow this might make my world better, happier; it might make up for the horror that has passed, if I adopt another child, one who's suffering, one abandoned and in need. Later, I will even suggest this to friends, speak of the idea as a genuine possibility. They stop me, of course, they make me get a hold of myself, and kindly but firmly guide me away from this irrationality. But for some time, the longing for another child remains.

I'm avoiding the eyes of these young mothers; I'm looking toward the restrooms. And a lovely woman appears. She has blonde hair, cut short, and fine, pleasant features. Her face is familiar. A moment passes, then comes the recognition, how much she looks like the woman killed by the man with the gun. So much so, I think, she could be her sister, but by that time, she's vanished from the park, she's nowhere to be found, and I wonder if I will see ghosts the rest of my life.

The next day I send the kids back to school, refreshed, more alive. My son's teacher calls me. She scolds me a little. She tells me authoritatively that children need routine, they need order, they need normalcy.

There's nothing to be said to this. I agree with her completely and hang up the phone.

The morning my husband died, my son, who soon began to dress all in black, took a stick of some sort, a hockey stick maybe, something strong, the length of his body almost, and started beating a cardboard box that sat on the kitchen floor. He beat it hard, as if it were a rabid dog he had to kill, his face blank but determined, his hands gripped in fists around the wooden pole.

Someone stopped him. Someone said, *No, you mustn't do this,* and took the stick from him and led him away.

I am certain now that was a mistake.

Our will is a simple document, leaving the money, the house, the cars to each other, bequeathing jewelry to our girls, the Browning to our son, designating guardians for the children if we both should die. It is signed but not notarized, and therefore not recognized by the state of Connecticut.

I wear a purple dress to meet my attorney at the Probate Office. It has grown too large for me, the dress; even my feet seem to slide around in my shoes. I arrive a little late. The attorney and the probate judge arrive later. We sit at a conference table in a stark municipal office. I can't tell you what business we conduct. Were there forms filed, documents exchanged? I have no idea. I recall only the judge's deep voice, and my attorney's elegant attire, the gold cuff links at his wrists, a different pair from those he wore at our first meeting.

The crank phone calls keep coming, I tell my attorney. The hang-up calls at all hours, the nuisance referrals, the long-lost acquaintances eager to show their concern and offer well-meaning advice. They frighten me, these sudden intrusions and unwanted intimacies, even telemarketers upset me. This is what is on my mind. Not money, not the paperwork of death.

He looks at a folder in his hands. He suggests solutions, an unlisted number, or caller ID. His wife had something installed, something done, to protect against that very thing.

And it pains me to hear him say, *my wife*. Of course, I scold myself, other people are still married. Other people still talk to each other late in the evening when the world is quiet, still love one another, still breathe the same air.

Other people's lives do not revolve around the slaughter on the bed of stone.

Those last words, those last few moments—I cannot forgive the universe for this.

At some point, I remember how to pray. At night I close my eyes, my energy slows, my body collapses like an empty suit of clothes. I let my worries fuel my invocations. I pray not to the blameless Christ who reigns in heaven, nor to God the Father, who is unknowable, unreachable, nowhere to be found. I pray to Mary, whose heart was broken on this earth for a design she couldn't possibly have seen nor understood. I pray for her guidance, for her human and mystical love to strengthen me and help me with my children.

And I pray to St. Jude, the patron saint of lost causes. I pray to him to grant me the desire to stay alive.

There are times, not every day as once occurred, but with a regularity still fairly shocking, in some lull in the hours, some dark settling of the dust of the soul, that I say to myself, as if reading from a newspaper report or over-hearing a passing conversation, *She couldn't take it any more, she put a bullet in her brain.* I think that still, now and then, the words coming back like the refrain from a sick, sick song. *She shot herself, she put a bullet in her brain, did you hear?* And I know I could do it, I've thought of it, where I might drive the car, how I'd get out and sit under a tree and not leave behind a bloody mess. And then the pain would be gone, my mind would cease its futile struggle to reassemble the scraps of horror tossing around in the blackness. I would be free.

But I have three children. I have responsibilities. And there's the hope, sometimes dismally vague, sometimes growing stronger, that one day I will move ahead.

Still, I have hidden my husband's revolver. I've wrapped it in an old shirt, buried it in a box and sealed it up. It's no coincidence that I haven't a clear idea just where the box might be.

I dream that we have moved to a huge old house. It's unfamiliar and empty, the rooms distant, darkened caves. The children are in their beds, and I'm awakened not by noise but by light, bright flashes erupting through the long, low window. In the distance, explosions burst in the dark, lighting the entire sky like fireworks, blooming like brilliant flowers. Nuclear explosions. A fearsome war has begun.

Somehow the morning comes, and the air is defiantly clear. I step outside the house into a lush, fragrant garden. Crowding the narrow path are tall, tropical plants, their leaves green as emeralds, heavy with some sweet, heal-ing fluid, larger than a pair of outstretched hands. Orchids bloom above me, red lilies float at my waist. I hear running water everywhere: a stream at my left, sculptured fountains just ahead.

Beyond the fountains, I see the colorful tents of a bazaar. Women in bright sarongs, their long black hair gleaming in the sun, lovingly tend their wares. They bend low over bowls of exotic spices, set copper pots in rows, nestle loaves of bread rich with nuts and honey into round baskets. A crowd dressed in outfits from another place and time mills busily about. Bearded men with turbans, children in short pants and tunics. A beautiful woman with a child in her arms. Some men are riding horses; some horses are wandering freely, their decorative bridles hanging loose. Gorgeous, virile animals, all but ferocious in their power, their brute sensuality, their potential to do harm. A single kick and you could be dead.

The air is heady with the perfume of flowers and fertile, wet soil. The sun is caressing and warm, magical, transforming. And I realize that I am naked. I am overwhelmed with the shame of my nakedness.

I am alone in a garden of earthly delights.

The men who knew my husband, who liked him well, who traded jokes and barbs with him around our pool table, who raised glasses of Scotch or beer in victory or, more frequently, defeat, who miss him now and worry about me, tell me there is a hell. They are certain of it, they are without doubt, hell exists; there is a place or a time or a state of mind in the afterlife, a horrifying moment or maybe an eternity of reckoning. They tell me this, their faces carved with conviction, their eyes boring into mine or sharply focused over my shoulder, I can be assured, I can trust, I can have faith. Justice will be served, justice will be meted out, by a God who sees all and remembers, by the universe itself, perhaps, but it will be done. The man with the gun comprehends the suffering he has caused, he knows it like he knows his own name. He will live it out, live it over and over, experience it himself, in that hell, in that deathlike forever, or in the milliseconds of terror before all the synapses in his tormented brain ceased firing. He will be crushed under the weight of his own evil, see it in excruciating detail before his mind's eye, the unutterable depravity he has wrought.

I don't know whether to believe them, my husband's friends, my friends. I don't know if I want to believe, for to believe that the man with the gun suffers in kind is to have to think of him at all, and this I can hardly bear to do. To think of him gives him a semblance of existence, of humanity, of being, and I will not grant him even that, not even enough to damn him to endless hell—no, I will not give him a soul at all. He must have one, but I will not be party to it. Not yet.

But I have envisioned eternity for my husband. I have seen the afterlife I want for him, I can feel it in my marrow. He must have a hero's reward. There must be that recompense, a hero's celestial glory, his soul soaring through the stars, flying free. I think of scenes straight out of an astronomy text, supernovas exploding, the burst of neon colors against the black, the birth of galaxies at the far ends of space, and behind it all that mythic symphony, the music of the spheres, playing like a sound track for his enjoyment. I have seen it in a dream, this journey of his, his only fitting reward, and I want for him that peace and magnificence and serenity, I want him beyond the madness and cruelty that is the earth. I want that for him, even though it takes him away from me, farther every day, on his trek toward some rare and brilliant star. A place of wonder, I believe, of endless awe. A place of light and rapture.

I fear, too, that no matter how well I manage in this lifetime, what might be left of it, how well I bear it all, if I am successful and see these children safely into adulthood before my heart gives out, even if I do that, there may be no place for me under that extraordinary sun.

In time, I need to see the place where he died. I need to walk the path he ran, to see where he lost a shoe and fell; I need to feel the stone beneath my feet.

The man who lost his beautiful wife that morning in March takes me there. We've had lunch together, we've commiserated, we've become comrades of sorts, broken souls bolstering up one another against the undertow of grief. He drives me to the corporation but refuses to step inside.

The acting president was my husband's friend, I've known him for years. He sits behind his desk, a complete stranger now, and we talk, his eyes shifting about the room. I wonder if this is the desk beneath which he hid as the shots rang out, calling 911, identifying the shooter though he'd not seen the gun in his hand. And I wonder if he thinks he is fit to serve in my husband's stead.

Before me is a copy of a brochure the corporation wants to display in gas stations and convenience stores and on bank and supermarket counters all across the state of Connecticut. Their message is solemn; their purpose, to encourage people to give money to me and to my children, and to the others who have lost their loved ones, too, to help us, it reads, meet our future financial responsibilities. The names of my children are listed on these leaflets, my name too, all of our names, with a little line by each one to be checked off or not, designating the donations, the amounts, the lucky recipients.

The acting president tells me, as if I haven't any sense, as if can't judge for myself, *It's all done very tastefully.* His eyes never meet mine.

He must be insane, I think. Clearly, they must *all* be insane, whoever came up with such a humiliating piece of work, whoever wrote it, produced it, without even asking my permission. Ott would be horrified, I tell him. I am horrified. Why on earth would I want my children used in this way, trotted out like circus ponies for a charity draw? Why I would I want strangers all across the state to think I can't pay my light bill?

I won't go along with it, I say, I won't be part of this, of what to me is an obvious public relations effort, an advertising campaign meant to put a good corporate face on mass murder.

But they've been printed, he says. Thousands of them. They're ready to go.

I am not moved. "Then you'll have to throw them out."

The young attorney joins us. He'd made that terrified sprint to the parking lot with my husband, he ran alongside him, then continued farther on, to the very edge of the wood. The conversation ends, and together, we all step out of the building. It's a long walk, longer than I'd imagined, around a bend, then deep into the gravel lot. The attorney tells me, when I ask, *Here, here*, and we pause. I don't remember if anything else was said. Tall trees surround us, the air is quiet, the morning disarmingly peaceful. A few cars pass slowly by, and I wonder if their drivers remember, if they ever say a prayer as they go.

And I'm relieved by the visit. I know my husband is not here. He is not on the bed of stone. Nothing of him remains in this dismal, deceiving place, not hanging in the air around us, not trapped in the earth or in the roots of the weeds along the side of the road. Thank God, thank God, he's not here. I've brought three beautiful roses, not pink, not coral, but something in between, the most unusual color, and I set them quickly at my feet, marking the spot, and pick up a handful of stones and stuff them into a pocket. Later when I look at them, I see splotches of red against the gray.

That afternoon, rain falls in torrents, a thorough cleansing, hours of sheeting downpour, thunder rocking the earth and sky. And I realize that I'd forgotten to take the flowers out of their florist's wrap. I'm ashamed of myself, of my stupidity. In a rush to leave, I'd simply set them down on the gravel; to anyone else they'd look like garbage, like a tossed-out sack, not the fitting remembrance I thought they might make, three perfect and unique roses tied in a ribbon, one flower for each of our children.

The card I'd left pinned inside will never be read.

That night I speak with the corporation's chairman of the board, a quiet man my husband liked immensely, a man who will soon be gone from this sad duty. He tries to change my mind about the brochures, tells me their intentions are honorable, that they'll raise money we might one day sorely need. I sit in the dark of the dining room, the heavy gold chandelier hanging unlit above my head, telephone receiver to my ear. I hear him out, but he knows it's a waste of his good time, and he doesn't make much of an effort.

Already, I am nearly lost to the corporation.

The police complete their report and, in an act of gallant public relations, the commissioner of public safety invites the surviving spouses to review that report with him. We each get an audience, a private session, and I know I'm supposed to be touched and comforted by this show of compassion. But I've had all the smoke and mirrors, all the posturing of politicos I can stomach. I want honesty. I want the whole story.

And I know before we meet, I've read it in the newspaper, that the report itself is incomplete. The detectives don't interview the psychiatrist of the man with the gun. They chart the scene, they photograph and record. They interview the killer's family, his friends, God knows how many from the corporation, but they don't talk to the man who treated him for depression, who medicated and counseled him since the previous fall, who approved his return to work after a three-month stress leave. No, they don't bother to interview the shrink. They don't ask him a thing.

I am predisposed to dislike the commissioner, and nothing he does in my presence amends my opinion for the better. I meet him in a police head-quarters' conference room, my attorney at my side, a copy of the report in front of me, a slender account bound snappily in red. It's not all there, of course, none of the interviews themselves are within those covers. It's a summary of sorts he gives us, a surface-skimming, semidigestible synopsis of mass murder.

The commissioner is talking to us, there's a small group assembled, a man from the state's Office of Victim Services, a deputy, perhaps, another face or two across the table, I can't accurately recall. The commissioner's lieutenant sits nervously at his side. The room feels crowded, cramped as a cell. We're tossed into this small space, the walls closing in, the air hanging heavy and toxic, charged with my own rage. I flip the report open and shut before me, recalling my attorney's counsel to be calm. He's told me earlier this sort of meeting almost never happens, that we should just take what they give us and be appreciative at this point, we shouldn't make waves.

I am dressed in a favorite ensemble that helps me remember who I used to be, a woman with a backbone, a woman with resolve. I wear that morning my best blue silk suit with a short skirt, silver jewelry significant as talismans, snakeskin three-inch heels. It is not in my game plan to remain entirely meek.

"Whose decision was it to *not* interview the psychiatrist?" I ask.

The commissioner balks, but only briefly. It's a question for which he's ready, he's anticipated this one, he's taken a short moment to prepare. He tells me straight-faced, simply, without embellishment or change in tone, as if speaking to an idiot child, that it was a decision made by *the police*.

I look at him, unkindly, I'm sure. Aren't *you* the police? I think. Just say so, you gutless jerk.

"The job of *the police*," he continues quickly, on a roll, "is not to investigate motive, but to determine that a crime has been committed."

Given that five people are dead, determining that a crime has been committed couldn't have been much of a stretch. But I don't say anything, I don't vent my feelings, I remember my attorney's sound direction, and for now, for once, I follow it.

Nonetheless, the lieutenant knows I'm furious. He's so uncomfortable he can't look at me, and I feel sorry for him, sorry he's been trapped into this stunt. And, deep down, I am sure the commissioner is a fine man, too, a good family man, his children must adore him; I'll bet he's a helpful neighbor, and gentle with his dog. But I can't stand the sight of him. He's just one more bureaucratic prig who, instead of doing his goddamn job the way it ought to be done, has planted himself and his office between me and the truth about what happened to my husband.

The families of the victims are not entitled to copies of the interviews, or the crime-scene photos we needn't see to believe, or any of the other copious, substantiating evidence, none of which is suitable for public consumption. However, we are invited, the commissioner declares, to make an appointment to come into the office at another time to view them. It is an invitation I will decline.

"We'll get the rest of the report in due course," my attorney assures me after we leave. I trust him; they have their ways, attorneys, it's only a matter of time.

But I'm impatient. I'm miserable and lost. I can't comprehend why my husband is gone, why nothing was done to prevent his death and the deaths of three other innocent people, how God and man alike could have allowed that unforgivable carnage on a gray Friday morning in March.

I put getting a copy of those interviews on my own list of things to do.

My dear friend from Delaware, the wife of my husband's boyhood pal, his golfing and hunting buddy, comes to visit, drives north from Delaware, spends too short a weekend with us. One of the kindest women I know, born on my mother's birthday, she shares with me a mixed Italian heritage, a love of home and family, and in our own disparate ways, the Catholic faith. She's a good Catholic, old-fashioned and devout, recites the rosary, attends Mass midweek and Sundays, hopes one of her gorgeous sons will grow up to become a priest. She is among the saved.

I pray for the intervention of saints and manage, on the occasional Friday morning, to sit quietly in the back of the church and not shake a fist at heaven. It's the best I can do.

One evening while she is with us, we take the children out to eat, to a darkened, too quiet restaurant. In a lull in the service, my son rocks and nearly topples the table, my daughters squash the miniature coffee creamers with their fists, sending spatters of milk all over themselves and the high-backed benches, creamy droplets landing in everyone's dark hair. Sugar packets become grenades. None of this amuses me; I try and fail to rope in the kids, *be still, be still.* Finally, the food arrives and we feast, and for a while, forget ourselves.

Later, my friend and I sit in the game room at home, polishing off an acceptable Chianti, the children settling into their beds. The venom pours out of me, an overflow of hate, rage, disbelief. I know too much to pretend that what happened couldn't have been prevented. I know too much to keep from picturing in my mind those last three seconds. I want the people responsible for Ott's death—the useless bureaucrats, the worthless shrink—I want them fired from the jobs they so pathetically fill. I want them exposed, humiliated, disgraced. I want them begging for their lives, I want them ruined, I want them to know down to their bones how it feels to lose everything. There is no mercy in my soul, no light, no grace. I am like the walking dead.

She sits near me, and she says. "He suffered. He suffered, and now you are suffering."

"I don't feel him anymore," I say. I have, I have felt him near, everywhere in this house, hovering about in the kitchen at the dinner hour, standing close as I walk the drive to retrieve the morning paper. But something has changed, my world is so dark, my mind so distressed, he is beyond me now, beyond my grasp, beyond the reach of our miserly human senses, of touch, sight, sound. "I don't feel his presence around me."

I've had a lot to drink. A good friend lets you go on, even if you've had a lot to drink.

"It must be beautiful on the other side, don't you think?" I ask. "Beautiful, peaceful. Not like the earth at all." I look at her, finish the last of the wine. "Why would he even want to come back?"

My face must tell her to find me a reason. "He'll be there when you need him," she says. And I believe her, she'd never lie to me, she's never said a callous or untrue thing in her life. And she adds, as only she would know how, or that I need her to, "He adored you."

We say good-night. I see that the guest-room is ready, make sure clean towels hang in the bath, and then I slip into bed. I don't know if I pray or cry or dream. Probably the prayers and tears and dreams are all used up for the day, for the week, for a lifetime. But I do sleep, soundly, restfully, until early morning.

I hear my name. I open my eyes, sunlight filtering into the room in a gray-gold haze. I hear it, resounding, sharp, practically a shout. "Neci!" In my husband's voice, though low and alarming, as if meant to carry across a great distance, the name only a handful of people in the universe call me. "Neci!" Loud and clear, unmistakable. And I am fully awake, the dark furnishings of our room—the bureau and its tall mirror, our wedding photo on the wall—taking shape before my eyes, colors clarifying, deepening yellow, green, rich brown. My heart beating again, my lungs filling with what feels like their first grateful breath in ages, my body still and snug beneath the covers. Comforted. At peace.

I am awake, and I hear.

Love survives.

3

A Distant Shore

MAYFLIES SWARM IN THE DARKENING AIR OF EVENING, THOUSANDS OF THEM tumbling together, a riotous, brainless sprawl and surge, fornicating like the flood of a river to the sea.

Suddenly, it is late spring. Somehow the ground has thawed beneath the gravel, the sun grown hot and immediate, the sky turned a melting blue from gray. The neighborhood revels in the bright yellow green of new growth, in the sturdy balcony of heavy branches overhead, in pampered flowers thriving in bark-mulched beds. Purple azaleas bloom beneath scrubbed picture windows. A fleet of children's bicycles comes out of hiding, bringing on the cacophony of a suburban parade. Our gated community pool, in all its chlorinated glory, opens to its tidy membership.

The children's school year comes to a close. The fifth grade plants a tree in Ott's memory. At the announcement in the crowded auditorium, my son asks if my tears are tears of joy or sorrow. It's too soon for joy, I say. But even a child is aware that something's changed, a firm, squared furrow in the ground has been marked and measured. That first long season of sadness has come and gone.

The good neighbors two doors down stop by, carting gifts for the kids, a net for the naked basketball hoop looming over the drive, a framed picture of Mickey Mantle for my son. The husband pulls the ladder from the garage, hangs the net, then rakes the rotting leaves and muck out of the clogged gutters. And later we adults sit at the kitchen table, sipping bloodred Chianti, trading cheerful news of family, and they tell me of a man they think I ought to meet, when I'm ready, when it's time.

Only rarely, only to myself, do I say what I miss, what I want, what I need. A caress, a touch. A man's arms around me again, his grip tight and strong and doubtless. Winding myself around his body like a child climbing high in a tree. Running my fingers along the line of his jaw, in the fine hair at his temple. Kissing his lips and the hollow at the base of his neck.

I'm only a woman, after all.

I let myself imagine someone. A stranger, a lover, a friend. I am leaning into his embrace. I am opening my mouth to meet his. And I recall the closing lines of a letter I received long ago, one I've never discarded, not through marriage, through love and loss, the stretch of time and too many miles. *I kiss your lips, your eyes, your hair,* the man wrote to me, from across an ocean, from another life. I can see his handwriting in my mind; I can trace the dark ink on the unlined page. *I long for you.*

I imagine hearing the words spoken. I imagine the rush and need. But to say it, to think it even, seems weak and foolish, a frightening thing. To know that twisted deep within that longing is a suffocation, a certain drowning, a cold and relentless desire for death impossible to confess.

Love is awful, I write in my journal. *Love is a cruel joke played upon us by a crueler God.*

I was twenty-five when we met, holding down an inches-above-entry-level clerical job in state government in lower Delaware, spending my days entering payroll and pension data into a gray computer screen. He was the new budget analyst on an upper floor, a well-dressed and cheerful addition to the lunchroom, with a great physique and a brilliant smile, a pair of amber-tinted aviator sunglasses shading dark eyes. He drove an immaculate white sports car and created an animated buzz among the single women. He was quite simply the catch of the day. An evening accounting course I had no interest in but thought might eventually push me up the depressing employment ladder on which I found myself gave us our first chance to take a close look at one another. I liked what I saw but said nothing. He kept his distance and said nothing as well.

I worked for a man for whom the polyester leisure suit with the expandable waistband had been invented, the size of his mind a direct inversion of that of his girth. I hated my job and knew I had to get myself into graduate school. I'd earned a BA in English literature, honors and all, Phi Beta Whatever, and it had prepared me well for a career in moving memos and data sheets from one side of a cold steel desk to the other. I was killing time, living at home on my parents' farm, saving a little money, paying off the loan on a new-but-stripped-to-nothing Toyota, heading down to clubs at the beach with girlfriends at the end of the workweek. My postcollege dating history consisted of a string of attractive users and idiots, and I'd grown bored and depressed with the whole thing, with the primping, the small talk over mediocre chain-restaurant meals, the obligatory fumbling in the dark. For a while I went out with a good-looking bodybuilder and gambler of some renown, who had his qualities, I'll admit. Conversation wasn't one of them, but he was fun to watch at the racetrack. Still, I longed for something more, and when he signed my birthday card, "Your pal," I cashed in my chips.

One late spring day, the Catch was getting on the elevator, heading up to his office somewhere above me. And I said, as I passed the open doors, barely looking at him, barely thinking at all, "That's a great car you have." A stunning opening line. I walked on.

He called after me. "You'll have to go for a ride sometime!"

And I said, "Sure."

When I stepped back into my windowless, standard-issue office, the telephone was ringing.

There was no way he was getting married again, he let me know, over our second, calculatingly casual lunch date. And I considered that, very much wanting a husband, wondering if this man was just too old for me anyway, almost sixteen years, and a little too cocky, a little too flip. But he was simply the nicest, smartest guy I'd ever dated, always upbeat, game for anything, and gorgeous; even when the car radiator blew up in his face, I wasn't worried. What's a little scarring, I thought, thank God he closed his eyes.

And he kept calling, and our dates became standing; he kept driving hours from his upstate home to take me to *Star Trek* movies and to dinner at good restaurants and dancing at nightclubs I suggested, to Rehoboth Beach for days in the sun, and for an afternoon ride on the Cape May–Lewes ferry when I offhandedly mentioned it might be a hoot. He left no doubt, though, the institution of marriage had lost its charm for him, he was not interested, not at all. A long year passed before he confessed he'd been married twice already.

A stroke of good fortune tossed me into graduate school at the university in Newark, and I took an apartment with a college friend. Ott and I kept seeing one another, most evenings, all weekend long. I studied postmodern fiction and Shakespeare's tragedies and taught remedial English and freshman composition. He came to poetry readings and commiserated when I cried over the nightmare of a thesis I'd never complete. And he gave me a Seiko watch for my birthday.

My parents were concerned. They'd worked hard all their lives—my father in insurance, then later as a teacher and farmer; my mother, an expert seamstress, and always busy helping dad—and were making plans to retire and leave the state. They wanted their dreamy-headed daughter who'd never keep herself above the poverty level well and safely married off. And Ott, they'd come to think, was just a much older man dragging his feet, stringing me along.

I knew better. I knew he loved me. I certainly loved him. I loved Saturday mornings together solving the crossword puzzle in the paper, and scrubbing silverware and roasting pans at his parents' house after Sunday dinner. But I was disappointed. I wanted the fire I found in poetry, proclamations of undying devotion, and a big, shiny diamond to glitter in the moonlight and show off to my girlfriends. I set a mental deadline. Christmas was it, or he was history. There were lots of single men at the university, among them a particularly cute Canadian. I could live in Canada.

On Thanksgiving morning, Ott came into my room and woke me with a great laugh and slipped the three-quarter-carat diamond ring on my finger. I phoned my parents immediately. A great sigh of relief sounded from the angels in heaven, and my mother's patron saints intervening for us here on earth called home for their next assignments.

Years later, I'll teasingly teach my young daughters to hold out their arms wide and say, "If you want to marry *me*, you have to buy me a *big* diamond." It was a hit at parties.

We were married, nonreligious types that we were, in the pretty garden of a restaurant in my hometown on a scalding day in June, and honeymooned on Hilton Head Island, in an elegant condominium overlooking the water. I endured golf lessons, for which I hoped to earn a few gold stars. We drank Dom Perignon by the deserted pool and ate breakfast in our underwear on the balcony, and once, locked out, he shimmied down three stories to let me back inside.

A storm blew in, toward the end of our stay. Winds and rain brought down a few small branches, but otherwise little damage was done. Lightning snapped high above us, and the sky burned a brilliant orange behind the shadowed black of tall, blowing trees. The harbor waters shimmered and churned, scalded, enflamed. I took photographs for the meticulous scrapbook I kept in those days, precise borders on every edge, neat little captions under each frame. I hardly need to see those pages to remember.

What was he like? people ask, when they hear what happened, how he died, how long after I've stayed alone. They wonder what sort of man would do what he did, how he came to be who he was. Why I couldn't seem to move on.

He was larger than life, I sometimes hear myself say, and so he was. He had a way of filling the empty space in a room, he towered and enchanted, he never told the same story twice. He loved my cooking, pizza from scratch and fresh semolina pasta, and dry martinis made with Polish potato vodka, dirty jokes and busty bottle blondes with Southern drawls, and fine golf courses in cool, clear weather. He thought God was a flawed invention and a dangerous one, and that immortality lay in our children alone. He cried at the birth of his son and the death of his mother. He was altogether too attractive to other women.

He was an achiever, a doer, a winner; he played hard and fair and he hated to lose. At midlife, he missed the adrenalin rush of championship wrestling and motorcycle racing and sought it elsewhere. A dinner party might end in a marathon of "Trivial Pursuit" played for pennies. A round of drinks at the nineteenth hole rode on a slice into the woods. He cheered on his kids from the sidelines at soccer and Little League, and urged me to visit the driving range, to tackle the intermediate slope before I knew how to lace up a pair of ski boots. Once, when we were dating, I beat him at chess. He rocketed from his seat, flipping the board up in the air. We never played again. Many years later, I learned how to throw the occasional pool game that threatened to sour a Saturday night.

He was very political, one man of some authority said of him to the police, days or maybe hours after he was dead. *I don't think people liked him very much.* Another colleague, a woman who prospered under the subsequent president, said something of the same ilk, something venomous, those comments duly noted and recorded by the uniformed officers making their report.

I would come to read that report, of course. I marveled at the ease with which these resentful few spoke so ill of the newly dead. I have remembered the names of those two individuals. Years gone by, I remember still. It is safe to say that I do not wish them well.

They were very wrong, that man and that woman. A small trunk full of cards and letters, literally hundreds, sent in condolence attests to it.

We were married nearly twelve years. We had three children right away, our son, and then twin girls. I abandoned the doctorate in English literature to take care of them, a decision I made quite casually, with little regret and zero consideration for the consequences. Ott rose quickly in Delaware state government, then took an executive position in New York City, vice presidency in marketing for a gaming concern, and he stayed there all week, driving home Friday evening, leaving at dawn on Monday, stocked with dry-cleaned suits and pressed shirts. I managed things reasonably well alone. I carted our son to private preschool, changed untold diapers, made puzzles out of grilled-cheese sandwiches, lived through the chicken pox as it hopped from one child to the next, finally covering my own body with oozing sores and raising my temperature to 104. And I started to write again: poems, a few stories I'd send to little magazines, a novel that would not see publication.

With the New York job came the perks of privilege: an expense account for dinners out, an underwritten apartment in a complex he shared with celebrities, travel to London and Stockholm, and an ambitious, attractive assistant I was sure would sell her grandmother for taxi fare. She told him of the erotic dreams in which he starred, and once dressed up as an angel for his enjoyment, wings and halo and who knows what else. *Ott's Angels*, she and another coworker called themselves, parading into his office. All in good fun, he said to me, a little workplace levity, and I supposed I ought to be happy he told me at all. But when I saw the woman at a colleague's wedding, dressed in black, her lanky, backwoodsman husband at her elbow, she wouldn't meet my gaze.

Then, a year and some later, the good job was suddenly gone, with very little warning, eliminated through corporate takeover. Ott came home and played golf. For a few months, he consulted quite profitably in a Southern state. During the remainder of that long year, I watched our bank account dwindle and kept a gallon jug of cheap Chianti in the kitchen cabinet.

Finally, he took a job he didn't particularly want, and we followed him to Connecticut.

Was Ott your first husband? a close woman colleague, an executive from the corporation, asked me, after he was dead. We were headed out to a fancy dinner, this woman and two others and I. They were doing me a favor, getting me out of the house. *Was he your first?* I didn't understand the question, why she might ask such a thing, but something of it registered within. I wanted to throw a shoe at her.

I used to sleep with a man, I write in my journal. *Now I sleep with a pile of books.*

So that summer after he's gone, the men start to call. They ask me to coffee, ask if I need financial advice, tell me they are worried about me and they want to help, come to the front door and let me know their unappreciative wives are out of town visiting relations and won't be home till Friday late. Some are as lost as I am, I think; some are merely being kind; some have consulted the calendar and said to themselves, *He's been dead how long now? She must be dying for it.* And they call.

The world is full of lonely middle-aged men, and I'm an easy mark, an approachable little thing made all the more approachable by an obvious need of comfort in the face of crushing tragedy. I love men, I've always loved men, but it's too soon, too silly, or too hopeful, and a trigger to heartache when they feign friendship, when they pretend to see and know me as I am. How I long for that.

I do accept one invitation. I meet a handsome sergeant for a cup of designer coffee at a storefront café. We sit together at a small table against a wall, away from everyone else. He could capture starring roles with those features—the strong jaw, the intense eyes, the runner's physique. The mischief and hint of melancholy behind the brilliant smile.

But that's not why I've met him. That's not why he's here. He sets down his coffee and pushes a heavy manila interoffice envelope my way and says, "We thought you should have these." He tells me the papers inside are for my eyes alone. No one's to see them, no one's to know I even have them. Not my attorney, not my family or friends, no one at all.

We chat for a while, he asks me about the kids, encourages me when I say I hope to go back to school to finish the doctorate, reiterates snippets of our phone conversations as if cueing from cards under the table. Then he walks me to my car, teasing, "Don't drive so fast, okay?"

At home I open the envelope and lay the witness statements from that morning in March out on the bed. I read over them, unholy texts, working through the difficult handwriting, the smudgy photocopying, steeling myself to learn what the newspapers did not reveal. I review them again and again, until I know some passages by heart, until some pages wrinkle with tears.

Then I put them back into their envelope, slip the string around the circular stays, and hide them away in a bottom bureau drawer for many months.

"I miss Dad," my son tells me, rarely, quietly, as if he knows to say those words out loud will make me suffer more, or shout or cry, none of which he wants to see or hear again. He's taken to wearing all black; he's gained weight from feasting on the sweets I keep at hand, the ready solace for the small fry, and the fat-laden convenience foods I offer when I can't bear the kitchen duty on which I once thrived.

The week after Ott died, his briefcase was returned to me, along with his trench coat, framed photographs from the credenza behind his desk, a few boxes of awards that hung on walls. Inside the battered leather case was a small computerized notebook I'd given him, for keeping appointments, important numbers. *Low battery,* its LED panel would read when I tried to operate it, or an icon of a lock would appear. Or it would simply lie there dead in my hand.

I pull it out for my son. "Here," I say. "Try this, sweetie, I can't get the thing to work at all." He opens the case, touches one button, and the notebook fires right up, no power glitch, no password to navigate. And he smiles in utter delight, his eyes bright again, a bit of magic sparking a sad afternoon.

It seems a small thing in the retelling. But in those days, we lived for them.

Ott took an apartment in Hartford while he searched for a house to rent, and back in Delaware, I boxed up our belongings and painted every square inch of flat surface in sight. A posse of his best buddies came by to help him pack up the U-Haul, and early the next morning, in a steady rain, I followed behind with the girls and a meowing cat as he raced north in the truck, our six-year-old son riding shotgun at his side.

God help me, the house was ugly, the single unsightly construction in a community of mustard and mulberry colonials so large they could house municipal offices. A split-level atrocity, of a color I can't even recall, with a painful floor plan and stamp-sized kitchen. But it was home, thankfully only a rented one. Exhausted, we pulled mattresses and sheets and mismatched suitcases from the truck and readied for the night.

And later that week, the U-Haul unpacked and returned, furniture nestled against faded papered walls, boxes strewn about but slowly emptying, a few paintings hung on sturdy nails, I sat on the steps of the house, late in the afternoon, a little wine in a water glass. The children were exploring, running about the neighborhood, introducing themselves to the other children their inner radar detected, while I sat and daydreamed, knowing I ought to be with them, not able to rouse off the stoop. I remember that day, that warm April day, a haze of golden dust shimmering beautifully in the late afternoon sun, falling around me and everything in my sight, imparting a lovely glow. The air carried the gentle songs of birds, and now and then high, sweet voices, and laughter, too. A door closing snug and firm. A ball tapping against a paved drive.

And I remember—oh, I can see it so clearly, as if the woman I was still sits on those steps and dreams, as if she still exists—I remember thinking how very lucky we were to have landed in this place, underneath this protective dome of gold, inside this perfect bubble, this suburban sanctum. Surely no harm could come to us here, nothing bad could touch us now, we'd weathered the rough storms the sea had tossed our way, we had arrived. We were, I believed in my heart, I prayed to be true, finally safe.

We settled in quickly; the kids made friends; some mornings I had the other stay-at-home moms over for coffee and muffins. Even the kitty adjusted to his new hunting grounds, finding his way home by dark, disturbing only one neighbor, who met my husband in the driveway one morning as he grabbed the paper. Our cat has been trespassing, she said. She owned an expensive parrot, one she set out on the porch occasionally, in warm weather, to take the air. She couldn't allow the cat to wander onto her property. Something had to be done, the neighbor insisted.

Ott took the cigar from his mouth and said, "I'll have a talk with the cat."

Subsequently, we had few dealings with this neighbor. When her teenage son played in their backyard, I kept my daughters inside.

But we were safe, yes, safe, the only worries inside that miraculous bubble the threat of ice on power lines and heavy limbs, the touch of fever on a child's flushed face, the boredom hanging over the fading pullout sofa in the narrow den. Ott traveled a lot, or so it seemed. I tested new recipes in my tiny kitchen and wrote a weekly food column for the local throwaway, and found one woman, another writer, who would become, remain, a lifelong friend.

One day, for no particularly good reason, I chopped off my long dark hair to the nape of my neck, looked in the mirror, and cried.

We stayed in that house until the following April, when the owners broke our verbal agreement allowing us to finish the school year in one spot. They forced us out in order to sell, the snippy realtor documenting that I was uncooperative and a very poor housekeeper to boot. I took umbrage at that report; I was, in truth, merely mediocre.

I found another place to rent immediately—another holding station, more than an hour's drive away, but aside from the hefty travel time carting the kids back and forth to school until June, I wasn't unhappy to leave. That ugly house had never been my home.

And that was our life together in Connecticut, those early years, our moves from rented house to rented house, two mid-school-year adjustments for the kids, my husband's disappointment in the job, his trips to New Mexico and the Philippines in search of something else, someplace better, trips that didn't pan out. The late night call to my parents when I'd finally had enough, when the feeling of being carted about like a Formica-topped table had gotten to me, when I played house alone through one-too-many industry conferences, when I knew all I cared to know about the adventure-some saleswomen who visited the office, sporting no underwear, the advertising and vendor reps who traded their tired, voyeuristic divorce stories and God knew what else for steady contract renewal. When I knew after so many years of marriage and motherhood, what a fucking bore I had become.

You have to do what's best for the children, my father said into the phone, quite forcefully, a directive he feared I might not take. My mother got on the line and said the same. And so I did. I did what had to be done.

So those two years passed, as years tend to do. I wrote another unpublishable novel, I kept the house, kept the children clothed and fed. I saw friends for lunch. That summer in the second ugly rental, I felt we lived in separate worlds. I would stand on the raised deck, standing outside of my very existence, wishing I were anywhere else. I suspected my husband wished the same. I never believed he'd been unfaithful, only that he had ample chance and cause. I was selfish and small in the destructive ways the insecure can be; I didn't know how to make things better, and quite frankly, didn't feel it was entirely my job. I escaped in dreams. I imagined another life.

An opportunity to travel came my way. And on the overnight trip to another city, I met a man I'd long admired. He told me I was beautiful, which I liked, and brilliant, which I liked even better. And I came home knowing what I was capable of, and what I wasn't, and what I wanted most of all.

Sometimes a woman has to be very clear, most importantly in her own mind. *Figure out what you want,* my good writer friend instructed me, *or someone else will figure it out for you.*

Things began to change almost immediately.

I know you could leave me, he said. *I know you've been unhappy.*

I didn't want to leave. He was my husband, my lover, the father of my children. And I loved him, quite desperately, and there was no one I desired, wanted, or needed more. I loved him, I loved my family, but I longed for a marriage worthy of us. I longed for a real home. I wanted to put down roots, preferably in this hemisphere. I wanted our lives together to begin anew.

And he made the effort to please me, then, to keep me maybe, or to keep us whole, and he showed me his intentions in the ways he knew best. He bought me the biggest, loveliest house I'd ever lived in, and one day not long after, showed up in the drive with a shiny new Volvo and said it was mine. And we'd join a country club, too, he said, hoping I'd learn to play golf, so we could play together. I said, *Of course, yes,* though I've always liked that definition of the game as "a good walk spoiled." Yes, I would learn, happily. I thought it was an excellent plan.

He planted tomatoes in the backyard, puttered through the chores of setting up house, singing dirty songs to make me laugh. *Gonna tie my pecker to my leg, to my leg! Gonna tie my pecker to my leg!* I filled my new sunroom with geraniums and succulents, and loaded the kitchen bay window above the sink with African violets I fed drop by drop out of a purple bottle.

"You love those violets more than you love me," he teased.

"Only a little," I said.

For a short, sweet while, we lived the American Dream.

So it wasn't all moonlight and roses. It wasn't a decade-long catered cruise on smooth seas, orchestra playing on the far end of the deck, good wine overflowing our cups. It was a marriage, probably very much like your own. Barbecues, surprise parties, vacations with friends. Dishes in the sink and the list of Saturday errands. Soccer matches in the cold autumn rain, Christmas Eve gift-wrapping marathons after the kids were asleep. Deaths in the family. Anniversaries spent apart. Hangovers the long morning after when it wasn't worth it. Naughty behavior under the cover of restaurant tablecloths. Arguments in the car on the way home. Mistakes, and the appalling, vital lessons learned from them. Passionate, wordless reunions. Finishing each other's sentences over weekday dinners.

An ordinary marriage. Getting better, growing stronger, despite it all.

We were on our way.

We were going to make it.

And then one Friday morning, he was simply gone.

I dream of the man with the gun. He is terrorizing a young woman, and to divert him, I yell, throw rocks, and then he comes after me. I jump into a car, and he climbs behind, into the backseat, and grips my throat with his hands. And I'm terrified, I start to drive, try to hold him off with one hand while I steer with the other. I know he will kill me, I know I can't escape, so I decide to kill us both. And I do this, slamming the car into buildings and stone embankments until I am quite dead, and he, too, I assume.

Then all my senses shatter and collapse. The struggle is over, and in its place, an unearthly peace has settled. My eyes open anew. Colors fall around me like broken pieces of glass, like a gentle tumbling of images out of a huge kaleidoscope, and in time I realize I am under water, pleasantly suspended in a warm, blue-green haze. I see myself swimming like a fish, as if I were born to it, diving far down, searching for something beautiful on the bottom of the sea.

He is at peace, that close woman colleague of Ott's tells me over that dinner. She's had a dream of him, and in the dream, he came to her and told her this. This is the woman's way of telling me, among other things more subtle and disturbing, that I should be at peace as well. I should seek peace. I should lay aside my bitterness and grief.

I know it would be better for me, or at least so much easier on everyone else, if I could follow her advice. But peace is a foreign concept, a state of mind I will find for many years only in dreams, in memory, in comforting visions of the sea.

And the day does come when it is all too much, when I can't bear it another minute, when his last moments are as clear in my mind as the bright summer sky, as real as the emptiness of my hands, when my failings rush over me like a cold blast off the water. *Get in the car, kids,* I say, and off we go, not sure where, on winding roads through the beauty of Northwestern Connecticut, out of the calm, bucolic development where I am rapidly losing my mind, out of the orderly intersections and adequate parking and easy access to new construction of mini malls and video stores and high-ceilinged chain restaurants, out of the familiar, the awful, the claustrophobic, the high-end avenue of despair. And we drive off in a new direction, off for an afternoon adventure. Maybe we'll stop for lunch, maybe we'll ride forever.

And in the heart of utter nowhere, set back from a tree-lined country roadway, we come across a huge toy store, a child's dream of heaven in the middle of a hayfield. The kids sprint inside, they travel the aisles in sheer pleasure, speedily assessing the merchandise, pointing at racks high above their heads, running eyes and hands over electronic games and action heroes, stuffed puppies the size of sturdy ottomans, bean-filled animals the girls already collect and carry about in their pockets like talismans. Their faces turn up at me, again, again, gleeful, smiling. Like the faces of ordinary children.

You want that? I say. *Sure thing! That too. And that.*

And we cart the bright armfuls of loot up to the front of the store, set it out on the low wooden counter, several hundred dollars' worth of molded plastic and Japanese robotics, lilac pile and round glass eyes, whole notes and rainbows at the touch of a button, the best-spent money of my life.

In the afternoons, I take the children to the community pool, where they meet their friends, and the mothers of their friends, who give them the easy smiles I cannot, who have remembered the floating devices and plastic rings for tossing games and extra towels for when the first is soaked through. I tote a bag full of papers and books, sit along the fence in my shorts and sun-glasses, and take notes on the novels I hope will make for a promising PhD proposal. Returning to school is the only way, I've told myself, to secure any sort of future. I've found a champion at the university where I'd studied, the frenetically brilliant Byron scholar, the former graduate chair, and he's en-couraged me, given me strength, greased every obstinate wheel for my speedy return. I'll study Russian as my second foreign language, analyze works on the Holocaust for the dissertation. On those summer afternoons while the children swim, I devise what I imagine to be a wholly workable plan.

No one has to know that mixed in the chilled bottle of soda settled in the sandy soil beside me is a healthy shot of vodka. No one has to know how much I need it. No one, to be honest, comes all that close to finding out.

One afternoon, though, a beautiful woman walks toward me, an angelic figure, slim and fine-boned, graceful, tall. She knows who I am, she's seen me sitting alone, she says, as if I shouldn't be. She tells me her name, says her husband is a doctor, they live nearby. Her voice flows softly, her words car-ried along on a sweetly accented South African song, asking after the kids, wondering how I am, without prying or intrusion, you can see it in her eyes, hear the kindness in her voice, the simple hope that we were well.

I imagine I told her we all were very well, indeed, we were all just fine. That is what I told myself. I don't recall the conversation beyond those lines, if I thanked her, if I even thought to ask about her own life. But I remember this woman for her genuine concern. It seemed a rare thing by then, and I have remembered, I have wished that lovely stranger well.

I dream again and again of him standing before me, displaying his wounds, his hip, his temple, the back of his head. I dream of reunions too sweet for this earth, aching and keen, my senses bursting open in an unpar-alleled joy. And I wonder, more often than I admit even to myself: if I knew for sure, if death would bring me to him, would I give up on life for good?

Life is for the living, so a friend sweetly says, his voice a gentle song on the telephone line. He offers a story of sadness he's known, of how he endured, he tells me I'm young, I'm attractive, I'll be happy again. He tells me I must.

L'chaim, he says, as if raising a glass, he says it again, so I'll not forget. *L'chaim*.

I record this in my journal, without remark.

When my mother and father were newly married, not long after the war, they lived in an apartment house in Forest Hills. A man and a woman lived next door, on the other side of the thin wall. I don't know how well they knew each other, my parents and this foreign pair, if they met in the halls and nodded, if they shared anything more. *They had that look,* my father says. *You didn't need to see the numbers tattooed on their arms.* And every night they sobbed together, the man and the woman, on and on, their cries carrying through the walls, weeping for those they loved, for the many they'd lost in the camps.

As a grown woman, my husband gone but my children safe in their beds, my own fine house quiet and secure, by chance late at night I sat in front of the television and learned how a young girl had survived. With her good friend, she'd made a bet. They'd have strawberries and cream after the war was over. They'd live through it, and together they'd have bowls of sweet strawberries and cream. And on the endless march in the bitter winter cold, her beloved companions freezing to death in a few hours' sleep, the snarling shepherds, the loaded guns, the heavy-booted Nazis at her side, she let herself imagine strawberries and cream, and the party dress she'd wear as well. Would it be red or blue? From what cloth would it be cut? She gave herself over to long reveries, to her iron-willed imagination, she made her escape in the only way she could, and she survived, though her good and beautiful friend died in the ice, though there was no one left with whom to share the strawberries and cream.

That good friend, before she succumbed, whispered to the one who would carry on, *I'm not mad at anybody, and I hope nobody's mad at me.* Those last words etch in my mind; they chastise me, the knowledge that a young woman who'd lost so much could find within her compassion, forgiveness, peace.

A very long while will pass before I see even a trace of those qualities within myself. Grief and anger turn me to stone.

Four in the morning and I'm sick with worry, numb with guilt over my many failings, with panic over all the difficult mornings to come, sitting curled up like a child in my husband's closet, the sobbing over, those worries hanging on, how will I hold it all together, how will I bring up three children alone, how will I provide? I review my sins, the missed athletic events, the greasy take-out dinners, the bedrooms that haven't seen a vacuum or dust rag in a month and a half. And my prospects, the nearly useless master's degree in English literature, the uncertain road toward a doctorate, freelance writing revenues that wouldn't keep us in paper goods. An indemnity less than one-half of Ott's salary, one for which I'm grateful down to my soul but fear could evaporate at a politician's whim, or a bad turn in the economy. I trust no one, least of all myself.

The corporation has promised to set aside money for the children's college educations. When the paperwork finally arrives, I'm appalled. I see the amount, enough to allow my kids to commute to the two-year technical school of their dreams, I think. What sort of promise is this, from a prosperous corporation, this shabby amount set aside in the names of its dead president's children?

I call the corporate attorney. *This is it?* I ask. *This is all?*

He's perplexed. There's a pause on the line. Maybe he's chosen the sum himself, the sum for which I ought to be appreciative, an amount meant to cover tuition at the state university. Not room and board, not books, but tuition at a fine school, an hour-and-a-half drive from our home.

It won't do, I say. It's crumbs, it's a token, it's another publicity stunt. I want more for my children, I want a good start, a decent education without scrimping. A promise has been made, not to me but to them, and I'm disgusted that I must ask that it be kept in full.

The garments of the silent, grateful widow never fit me well.

Our anniversary comes and goes. I buy a supermarket bouquet for the hall. Then Father's Day arrives, settles around us like a heavy mist we struggle through but barely acknowledge, the monstrous weight of knowing that in other houses, next door, across the street, there are tidily wrapped presents resting on polished coffee tables, charcoal grills glowing, ready for thick steaks, imported bottles of garnet-dark wine waiting open on the counter. It's a long day, and hot, filled with too many hours, like blank sheets of paper in a cheap notebook. The sky is a milky thing without a sun. In my journal I record the purchase of a black microwave oven, and the failure to find an American flag to fly in memory of the one not here, and little else.

I don't know what brings it on, why suddenly I need to have his belongings, the clothes he wore, his watch, his glasses, his shoes. A fear comes over me that they've been lost, mishandled. I make calls and requests, and one day a tall, quiet sergeant brings the large box to me, asks me to sign a receipt, tells me to call if there's anything else I need. I take the box down the hall to our room, set it on the bed. Inside are his possessions sealed in plastic, or folded carefully into paper bags, numbered, dated, described. His broken watch. His reading glasses, scratched and bent. The pen the governor gave to him upon signing the bill that, due to Ott's hard work, brought into being the corporation as it exists today.

His clothes in their separate brown paper bags, the bloodied undershirt, the trousers, the socks, the tie. Whose blood, I wonder, knowing some of it could be from the man with the gun. I examine the fabric of each item, finding where the first bullet went into his hip, holding the clothing to my face, to my lips as if it were the palm of his hand, the hair at his right temple I kissed instead. And I fold each piece neatly, gently, like baby clothes set aside for the next beloved child, like heirlooms embellished with seeds of pearl.

And then I take his shoes, nestled in their separate sacks. I hold them in my hands. The good leather twisted, the soles deeply cut and scarred, scored as if hacked with a knife, covered with a fine dust. And I understand then how hard he ran, down the center of that parking lot, how his feet dug into the gravel, how they pounded against the chipped stone. Until he lost his left shoe. Until he fell and could run no more.

The night his father died, we were living in a home we'd built on a piece of land adjacent to his parents', a wedding gift, several green, secluded acres in the middle of suburban sprawl. His mother had called, his father wasn't breathing. I was pregnant with the twins; I stayed with our son, still an infant, sleeping in his crib.

And he ran to help, down the length of fence in the October darkness, then through the fallow garden. Along the way, he lost a shoe.

I dream a lovely nurse in a crisp white dress is standing behind my husband's chair. He's seated in an old-fashioned wooden wheelchair, the kind you see in movies, in scenes of tuberculosis patients recuperating on the sunny lawns of sanatoriums. The nurse, I think, is washing his hair, or preparing to, gently bringing her long, slender hands to his temples. His eyes are closed, yet he seems revived, comforted, on his way to a cure through the warmth of her quiet, selfless care. As I come nearer, I see more clearly what she's doing. She's wrapping a strand of bright jewels around his head, across his right temple and in his hair. A strand of emeralds and sapphires and rich citrines, stones cut large and deep to catch the sun. A bandage of gold and fire.

One of my daughters, small and silky-haired, aged nine, sits with me on the sofa, watching a cooking show, one of the several I have fallen into the habit of screening like a reviewer, jotting down recipes, critiquing technique, lusting after the expensively appointed studio kitchens. A handsome French chef is folding molten chocolate into a rich batter, tossing jokes into the air as formidably as he works a silver whisk or spoon.

"He's funny, don't you think?" I say to my girl, giving her a little nudge and a smile. "Good-looking, too."

She leans a bit forward, examining the screen, her forbearance with adult programming seemingly unstrained. "He's okay. How old do you think he is?"

I laugh. "Too old for you, sweetie!"

She looks at me and counters, without hesitation, "I mean for you, Mommy."

During a weekend trip to Vermont to visit my brother and his family, and my parents, who have driven over from Maine, I watch my son trying too hard, trying to please, animated as a seasoned child actor under a bright stage light. He stands in the kitchen cracking jokes, serving up gentle sarcasm and quips, telling tales on teachers he was glad to say good-bye to at year's end. He's just turned eleven. He could be thirty, working a cocktail crowd of old friends after a shattering divorce, putting everyone else at ease. It breaks my heart.

My daughters dance to old disco songs my niece has turning in the CD player. They're into the music, under its spell, shimmying and shaking all in a line, then side by side, bopping to summer songs I remember belting out loud on the decks of seaside nightclubs I frequented when I was young. But the party doesn't last, the hour's late, the tempers short, and the voices rise over whose turn it is to play what, and my voice rises too, trying to contain the fray. My parents leave the room, too much for them. Too much for all of us. With that failure at my elbow, I find my way to bed.

In the dark early hours, I wake to the luxurious melody of steady rain against the windows, my mind focused not on my children, or on the family sleeping in other rooms, but on Ott, missing him, longing for him, wishing he could reach me, or I could reach him, on some plane of light and love I sense but cannot touch. I stop myself, unwilling to let others hear me crying, to spend long hours in tears. The heavy rain calms me, my body quiets, and I tell him over and over, *I love you, I love you, I love you.* I send it out like a song. Does he hear, does he know? Where has death taken him, how far beyond the grasp of human love does he fly?

And what if he's not free after all? What if disappointment, sadness, rage tie him here? What if he sees the chaos left behind at the corporation, his hard work unraveling through common politics and avarice, the posturing of legislators bent on greater name recognition, the painful questions about what went wrong that morning in March left unanswered?

It's then I come to believe that I have a duty, a task to complete, a charge to finish what was left undone. Someone ought to speak sharply to the flagging board of directors, to insist they steer my husband's ship into port. Someone must address the unacceptable loss of precious life. Lying there not quite alone, surrendering to the gift of rain against the glass, I think at least I ought to try.

You're just another media problem for the corporation, the advertising guru explains to me, as we talk on the phone back in Connecticut. I'm sitting at the metal desk, taking notes as I listen. I've asked for this man's advice, I've told him I must speak to the board of directors, and this pleases him, for there are things he'd like me to say, too. For eight successful years he's headed the agency that handles the corporation's advertising; he'd like another eight years, I can tell. We talk of the inflammatory articles in the newspaper, sometimes two and three a week, the reporter who haunts the board meetings and sounds the steady public alarm that in the wake of mass murder the corporation is out of control. A new chairman of the board has been named, and the guru tells me this is a good thing, though I can't follow the reasons why.

Tell the board you want to see them, he says. *They'll want a private meeting, no reporters, of course. Tell them not to be a punching bag for the newspaper, for self-serving legislators; tell them the corporation will not go away.*

He insists that I have the strongest place to stand on these issues, stronger than anyone else in the state of Connecticut, as the widow of the man who brought the corporation to life, who turned a flagging state agency into a quasi-public going concern, fiscally robust and booming. Perhaps the board will listen well, perhaps they will take my words to heart. I scrawl out four pages of notes, full of phrases like *budget cuts, contract renewal, negative political environment.* I write down everything he says. I know I'll only get one chance, and I don't want to waste it.

At the end of our discussion, though, after a few words on the children, after his reassuring blessings for the future, the guru gently counsels me, *I know you'll make a forceful statement, Denise. But it's not likely to change anything.*

Later, I phone a friend and tell him of my plans to speak to the board, the support I've received, my determination to set things right. He encourages me, my friend, envisioning a wild assault on the unsuspecting board members. He thinks I'm tougher than I am, and I like that; he asks if he can come along to watch. And he laughs: "Can I bring popcorn?"

Ott and I had made plans for a summer vacation, before he died, had booked a cabin for a week on Moosehead Lake in Maine, and arranged to meet my parents there, for they already loved the place, having discovered it in my father's wanderings through the wilderness. A family vacation. I had looked forward to it, reviewing the brochure in my sunny hothouse of a

Florida room, snow still covering the ground outside. And now, as the date nears, I dread making the trip without him. I don't want to go, but what I want doesn't matter. We need to get away.

We pack, prepare to leave, board the animals, secure the house. The drive, for me, is daunting, so I break it in two, stopping in Kennebunk at a lovely old resort. We settle into our adjoining rooms, then head out for the lobsters I crave, indulging hungrily, while at a nearby table a tall, dark-haired father entrances a gleeful child before their meal. It's too much to bear. My own children leave their seats to explore the tiny dock, and I sit with my back to the man, finishing my wine before we go.

Boats sway in the water steps away from our hotel, and I sit and watch them as a heavy fog rolls in. Honeymooners ask me to take their photo by a toy lighthouse. A boat owner pulls tools out of a wooden box, tightening something out of sight on the deck of a sailboat. I dream of being where these boats have traveled. I dream of being anywhere other than in my own mind.

At dusk, tiny insects appear, swarms of them zeroing in on bare arms and legs, driving us inside. We take refuge in front of the television until the hour is late, and then off to bed, but not before the children's bickering does me in. It goes on and on, relentless, infuriating, until I snap, I cry, I smack some-one's bottom once, I plead with them all to be quiet, to go to sleep, to give me a moment's peace.

In the morning, I'm spent. I'm an awful mother, I'm a failure, I'm that lump of ill-fashioned clay that didn't fire. I hold my children and kiss them and apologize from my heart. And my youngest daughter says to me, quite cheerfully, on cue of course, good and loving daughter she is, "It's okay, Mom. It was the right thing to do!"

That night, with the children finally quieted down, I suffer through the hours alone. I ask God, *Why didn't you take me? Let me be killed in an acci-dent, get sick and die off, useless empty thing that I am, let Ott carry on, he'd have done a better job, he'd have been the better parent to survive.* The television chatters on, a show about happy marriages. Humor and affection and good sex and mutual respect, the reporter says, are key ingredients. Some of the happiest marriages survive affairs. I drink this all in, record it in my journal, as if it were vital information lately learned, the birth date of a newfound friend, an appointment with a surgeon an hour's drive away.

Finally I sleep and dream, sharp images slapping me about. My son all in black, pounding on an electric guitar, shouting into a microphone. A bath-tub overflowing. A man I know, a would-be seducer, speaking Greek to adoring females. A blasting air conditioner sending shivers across my skin. I pull the cord and it snaps like a snake, sparks shooting up and around me. Debris falling in a slow-motion dance, like the insides of a globe of fake snow.

I wake gently, opening my eyes to the early light, to see a young girl sitting on the yellowed window ledge of my room, little more than an arm's length away. She's dressed like a flower girl in a fancy wedding, all in pretty white lace, a garland of delicate blossoms circling her head. And I think, *Why is my daughter here, why is she in the room? Is she sick?* And then I realize the figure isn't my daughter at all. It's not a human child. I scream out in a genuine terror, a shudder running through me, and I turn my face away and cry.

She smiled at me, the little girl. She smiled, as if at play, her golden head tilted, her tiny feet wrapped in white, hanging delicately beneath the hem of her gown.

When I turn back, the glimmering child, the apparition from another world, a vision of hope somehow still alive inside my own dark mind, is gone.

Later that morning, behind the wheel of the red Volvo, the trunk stuffed, the kids buckled into their seats, I remember a fragment from the night's many dreams. My husband and I are in the car together, we're off on an adventure, he's in the driver's seat. He puts on his amber-tinted aviator glasses, flashes me his brilliant signature smile, and adjusts his tie, or maybe I do that, I'm not sure. He's his handsome old self, we are our old selves together, as we once were, newly in love, looking ahead.

He clasps his free hand in mine, he holds it tight, up in the air, he gives my fingers a squeeze. And off we go.

Off we go.

There might be a more beautiful lake in the world than Moosehead, a view more hypnotic and calming, more gorgeous and unspoiled, but I've never seen one, and I wager I never will. The wide, lush lawn spills down from our comfortable cabin to the rocky water's edge, and across the expanse of hazy blue stand rolling hills, green and untouched, darker mountains beyond. The children run about entranced, spotting deer grazing lazily at the edge of the treeline and curiously tame squirrels begging for treats. My father puts on his hat and takes the kids for a hike, my mother retires to their lodge apartment for an afternoon rest. I walk the grounds unsteadily, as if feeling my way after a paralyzing siege, thinking how a few sheltered days in this hidden corner of the earth might restore me, how much in need I am of a kind nurse to wheel me across the rich green grass down to the water's edge in late afternoon.

His death never leaves my mind.

The serenity and the splendor, the unbearable peace of this place, terrify me.

The lake casts its spell. I get my bearings, I leave Connecticut behind. Something eases within, something opens up like the offer of an embrace. I remember to breathe, I remember to live, as they say, in the beauty of the moment. Sensual enjoyment right at hand. Lying in the sun blameless as a child, hearing the water tenderly lap the granite rocks. Falling in love with the sky at sunset—subtle hues, restrained and seamless—fading blues, grays touched with orange and pink. The mountains paled, hazed with distance. The water reaching a brilliant line of topaz at the far horizon, that distant perimeter unnaturally high in the clear, huge sky.

Geese lifting off the lawn, hundreds of them, honking, joining in a simple formation, alighting softly on the water, barely disturbing the surface, wings spreading wide as they land. Bobbing along the shore, submerging their heads, gray feathers glistening in the slanting sun.

Days so beautiful, they're nothing short of miracles. Days that give a body a reason to live.

The one book I've brought with me is a memoir written by a woman who's lost her beloved daughter after spending a year of torment by her bed as she lay in a coma. But it's not a book about that unbearable loss. It's an erotic cookbook, of all things, filled with sensual remembrances, lusty bits of history, recipes for South and Latin American aphrodisiac dishes. I read a few pages here and there, sitting in the sun on the cabin porch, feeling drowsy and content, daydreaming, believing that if this wonderful writer I've long admired could lose one so very precious and yet return to the world, to love, to joy, then maybe I could as well.

It's the first book I've read in five months.

One of the owners of the resort is a divorced father of two. He's an energetic presence on the lake, running about fixing things, tending outboard motors and stubborn faucets, making small talk after dark. He takes a shine to me, and why not? I'm the only ambulatory single female at or above the age of consent within thirty miles.

The sun's going down—would we like to go for a moose ride, take the boat farther up the lake, see if we can find a few big hulks grazing in the shallow water? The kids, my dad, everybody's invited, he says. And we bundle up, the day's grown chilly, and off we go; I sit right in the front, I relish the spray on my face, the wind in my hair, and it's wonderful, just wonderful to be out on the water, great gulps of sweet cool air filling my lungs. And I look to the man, who looks at me as he maneuvers the boat far back in narrow inlets, calling quietly to the kids, "Over there, over there!" as we come upon one huge bull turning his weight toward the low roar of the motor, raising his head to consider us through myopic eyes, then slowly lumbering toward the shore.

In the days that follow, I'm treated to jars of homemade jam, aromatic mugs of freshly prepared vegetable soup. The man builds bonfires for my children at dusk, takes my father fishing in the early morning hours, brings me a bottle of superb cabernet sauvignon, which we share over the course of a long evening together, sitting beneath the vast Maine sky alight with a million stars, watching the fire glow before us, telling each other our life stories. Revealing ourselves the way strangers sometimes do in the dark.

"No, sir!" he says, mimicking his ex-wife, the woman who broke his heart. "I'm not working, I'm not getting a job!" He stretches out his arms, leans back against imaginary upholstery. "I'm sitting *right* here!" In his real life, away from the lake, he's a merchant-marine engineer; one season out to sea, the woman didn't wait for him to come home. Now, he says, he spends his free time here, as much with his children as he can. For that evening he entertains me, he keeps me laughing, making sport of the brutalities committed within his own personal hell.

We tap each other's arms as we confide in one another, trade meager touches, and then he pulls me into a half embrace, tenderly kissing my hands, my cheek, my lips once, then my hair. We sit together a while longer, enjoying the warmth of the fire, the glow from the wine. When we say goodnight, he kisses my mouth; hesitantly and then quite expert, no stranger to the game, he draws me close to him, wraps his arms around my waist. I whisper that once I was an affectionate woman, once I was responsive, long ago it seems. He tells me he understands.

"When you're ready for life," he says, "I hope I'll be around."

We exchange a few letters, afterward—light, cheerful notes. He sends me photos of places he's been—Thailand, South Africa. He asks after the kids, says he hopes we'll come back to the lake. I do call the resort, once, when he's not there. But nothing more. I let the time, the chance, go by.

Years ago—I was so young, my face full, my brow unlined—I stood on a low bridge above a dark lagoon. A man walked below, talking to us, talking to the tourists who'd come to see the dolphins swim about the half-acre square of water. He was educating us, the man, the marine biologist, as he gave the dolphin pair simple commands and fish for treats after they were done. Twirls and jumps, quick relays from corner to corner, nothing strange nor elaborate, nothing unnatural. Elegant movements they knew by heart.

The man was a dark figure, at some distance, in the shadowed light at the end of the day. I couldn't make out his face or eyes, his height for sure, the color of his hair, but his voice was clear, nearly familiar, a cheerful pitch, I can hear it still. He picked me out from the others, from that half-circle gathered on the bridge, maybe it was his job, to play to the crowd a bit, to draw us in. He teased and called to me, "C'mon down!"

I laughed, pleased but embarrassed to be noticed. I shook my head, no, I couldn't, thank you, no.

"Sure you can. C'mon."

The day was still hot, the woman beside me fanned herself with a fold of paper. And I didn't go, didn't move from that safe perch on the bridge, not all those years gone by, afraid to step out from the crowd, to be singled out, to be seen and known. Even then.

Sometimes now, my life immeasurably changed, my wants and needs much the same as any woman's, I let myself imagine a scene, another sunset, another shore. I imagine another sky burning scarlet, the sea reflecting the flush of sundown, and a man I will come to know well building a fire from driftwood. The beach is rocky and wild, the water cold, but the air warms as the fire grows higher. Behind him the endless sky darkens, the water melts and disappears into that calm, flawless horizon seen in dreams.

C'mon, honey, the man says, his face and arms struck with angles of ruby and gold. He stands tall and holds out his hand, he says my name aloud. *Come on down to the water with me.*

4

Survival

IN MAINE, ONE UNCERTAIN HOUR WHEN THE GLORY OF THE LAKE AND THE endless sky could not comfort me, I scribble down a list—a long, sensible list—of things to do when we return to Connecticut, to our real lives. The priorities, the chores. Get the finances in order, see to the banking, get a handle on the monthly bills, the out-of-control credit card expenditures, the neglected investments. Talk with my attorney, if I can get the man on the phone; see about the taxes left undone. Call the corporation, the young lawyer, Ott's administrative assistant, too, check on the education funds again, and our medical insurance, how long will it last, under what circumstances might it stop, ask for documentation. Call a few old friends, too, keep in touch, don't let those ties fall away. Order printed thank-you notes (I'll never catch up by hand) and get them in the mail, quickly, five months have passed.

Buy presents for the girls' party, I write, but what party, what occasion, when and where, I haven't any idea now.

Added to the list is a simple catechism of sorts, a few philosophical questions, their plausible, practical answers suitable for those of limited insight, the devoted readers of paperback self-help books, the nearly gone. *How do you honor a murdered husband?* I ask myself at the end of the page, and in the narrow space that remains, reply, *Raise his children well. Insist that his memory, his work be respected.*

At the top of the list is another inquiry, the one for which the catalog of things to do has been created, and another concise response: *How do you get back the will to live? Work,* I say, is the solution. *Discipline.* I write these words simply, without further ado, as if I believe in them maybe, or want to, or found them hanging in the air before me, a slogan hammered out in wrought iron, arcing above an imposing gate: the *Arbeit Macht Frei* welcome to my own petty hell.

66

Then I ask, *Where does Love fit in with all of this?* And nothing follows this question, no answer appears, just a blank, a gap, an empty line.

So I return with a plan, with resolve, with that list to which I keep adding. It's not enough to deal with the tasks at hand, with the stinging debris floating in the orbit of our own despair. I reach outward, I try, I try. I'm all hours on the Internet, researching workplace violence, ordering books heavy with footnotes written by experts I've seen on morning talk shows, studying the Web sites of national organizations devoted to those who've been murdered, those left behind. I order a pamphlet entitled *Preventing Assassination,* and make sure it reaches the proper Connecticut authority. I search out the sick photos still illustrating the March online news stories, find one of my husband's uncovered body on a Detroit paper's Web site, and phone the editor in tears; she removes it by the next day. I request an appearance before the corporation board of directors for a date set in September, and schedule meetings with professors at the university where I expect to complete the doctorate. The head of an international organization, one of standing in the industry, one in which Ott had been active and an elected official, is a man I consider a friend, and I pester him to create a scholarship in Ott's name. And as the days shorten, the sunlight softens, I ready the kids for the start of school.

And it's all too much. By mid-August, I'm depleted, there's nothing left. I draft a report card of my own, assessing my mental and physical health, and my performance in the arts and sciences. In one area I give myself an *A: History. Remembering too much.*

It's now that friends lose their tact, their fear of offending me, they say how tired I look, how thin I've grown, ask how I sleep at night. They advise me outright to see a shrink, to at least keep an open mind. My good writer friend calls from her home out West, she tells me of her work, the lush garden of her own vibrant design. She cheers me on. And then, her melodic voice loving but firm, she gives me the name and number of a sensitive therapist in Hartford, an associate of an associate, a respected woman who sees only the survivors of murder victims.

I write the information down, of course, I file it away. I don't follow through. I don't heed the advice, the concerns. I've got too much to do.

What do *people do?* I ask the advocate from the state's Office of Victim Services, a bearded man with kind eyes and words, who's helped dozens of others through drive-bys and bar knifings and domestic slaughters alike. He's come to see me twice, has stayed patient with me at the glass-topped table in my pleasant sunroom, talking life and death. *What do they do,* I want to know, *afterward, when they see that no one else has done a damn significant thing, nothing's been challenged or questioned, the broken system stays fixed in bureaucratic cement, people are dead and the world carries on just as before? What do they do? Write books, run for Congress, set up foundations?*

How many times has he answered, how many times has he consoled? It's normal, the advocate says, to want to respond, to want to change things, to hope to channel the anger toward some good. He tells me of a homicide survivors' group that meets monthly, encourages me to give it a go, says he's sure I have some good ideas of my own.

I have plenty of ideas, and none of them good. I know I'm merely tossing pebbles against a high stone wall.

He tells me of a woman whose son was murdered in a bar, shot in the back for nothing, for a few harsh parting words, and after years of her waiting for the guilty verdict, the rich young killer, duly convicted, ready for sentencing, is let out on expensively obtained appeal. Away he goes, God knows where, gone, never to be seen again. In her heartbreak, the woman petitions the legislature, works hard to change the law that let him out. Because of her perseverance, no other mother in Connecticut will live through the same injustice.

A group of women in Stamford, survivors like me, he says, visits schools in teams and talks to young children, getting to them before they get to the guns. To succeed even once, I think. Even once.

More still have worked to help others through the nightmare of the criminal-justice system, to allow the victims' families more access and response, to attend hearings that once were closed, to be part of the process so finely honed to protect the rights of the accused. A process I am grateful to have been spared, thanks to the man with the gun's final shot to his own troubled head.

Sometimes, the advocate says, *after a murder, there are psychiatric issues as well.* I record that in my journal, not grasping the full weight of his words.

As we say good-bye, he tells me again the date and time and location of that next survivors' meeting, tells me to think about showing up, to think about the healing work that might be done. *You'll know,* he says, *when it's the right thing.*

I write in my journal the ordinary passings of the days, the cat chasing a mouse into a corner and pouncing, the girls' schedule at an exclusive soccer camp, their enrollment arranged and their tuition underwritten by an acquaintance, research conducted in the library for the doctoral proposal.

Notes for what I'll say when I appear before the board, reminders to pay the light and phone bills. A record of my too-numerous hours, mostly dull as double-entry accounting, interspaced irregularly with hysteria, with dreams too horrid to tell your mother, local phone numbers and no names to go with them. *Truffles, cookies, two for a dollar,* I've scribbled, half in a margin. *Friday. two o'clock.*

I draw a line as in geometry, arrows on either end shooting off into forever, and in the middle darken and label a short span, *fourteen years,* the length of time I spent with my husband. And I ask myself—there's no answer of course, but I ask— *What is fourteen years in the face of eternity?*

One morning I date the page and begin, before the mail arrives, before someone drops a teacup in the newly tiled kitchen or we pour bowls of cereal. I write, *Today I will not be sick. Today I will not drink like a fish.*

I imagine him stepping out of the shower, snapping the towel on his way to bed, his skin and cropped hair still damp, the smell of soap, the configuration of shoulder bones under the smooth flesh, the weight of his body against mine in the dark. I imagine him everywhere in this house. I pass him in the hall where he stands empty-handed, filling up space by the cellar door. I step around him in the kitchen while I'm cooking, or when I'm not but ought to be.

I feel him lingering near the window in the morning sun, as he did that first summer in our first home, our first baby just born, the kitten-blind boy he held gently to his chest, turning toward me to smile for the camera, our future nestled in the crook of his arm.

My daughters may have lost their father, but not themselves. That summer they see their friends, bounce around the pool and the soccer field, stage mini "Spice Girls" concerts with the neighbor's child, bicycle the shady block. Summer is freedom for them, and for me, freedom from schoolbooks and sitting still, from stale routine and too-early rising. The season buoys my daughters' spirits and reawakens something within; their mother benefits. Death has not emptied their reservoir of love; they are tender with me, returning the hugs I need so much to have returned, gifting me with crayoned cards and wildflowers pulled from the woods behind our house. Their sadness, or what of it I am aware, shows itself in quiet moments more than in tears, which fall, of course, now and then, most often at bedtime, in that idle, tired hour when the thoughts brushed aside during the busy day cannot be so well avoided. How often they keep those tears to themselves, I cannot know.

The father of the man with the gun plans to go to court to get the weapons. He wants the weapons his son used to commit mass murder returned to him, he says, so he can auction them off and give the money to the victims' families. He wants, it seems, to sell them to the highest psychotic bidders, to collectors of memorabilia of the morbid, to the sort of ghouls who might display the knife on a mantel like a brass candlestick, take the gun out of a locked cabinet to show dear friends who visit on the holidays.

I don't remember how I learn of this—if someone calls, my attorney, a neighbor, or if I open the paper one midmorning and find the story staring back, matter-of-fact and straightforward as a recipe for meatless lasagna, or an announcement of the opening of a high school play. But I remember a seizing up inside of me, a fear that wouldn't allow a focus beyond its grip. It comes back, that morning in March, it comes in the open window on the breeze of a warm summer day.

And it's a suitable topic for conversation, this pending lawsuit of the father's; you are somehow expected to hold a meaningful dialogue, to think about—to consider rationally and respond politely when inquiries are made—whether the gun used to blow your husband's brains out might one day be held aloft at a podium by a man brandishing a smooth and sanded walnut gavel, perhaps be available for preview a few hours before on the date of sale, or auctioned off worldwide on the Internet, maybe to some German neo-Nazi who'd best appreciate the beauty, the workmanship, of this particular model of Glock. It's reported in the paper, this lunacy, this disgrace, the father's suit. It's a current event.

And with the report comes an undocumentable knowledge, an inner sense this sort of thing will never truly end, like an illness that ravages your gut and doesn't quit, one no medicine can quite eradicate, one you simply can't shake.

I've seen a skinny old woman in the grocery store, I've watched her creep along the edge of an aisle, dressed for January at nearly the end of summer, empty hand-basket hanging from the tips of bony fingers, talking to the air about waxed paper. *Dear Jesus, dear God, dear Mary*, I think. *One day that could be me.*

I write in my journal, *miserable, miserable, miserable.* I hear myself repeating, at any hour of the day, *I'm tired, so tired,* and I know I must stop the despondent sound track playing in my head, I know the body believes everything you tell it, that I must take better care of my health, find some way to ease my mind, but there's no time, no energy for such nonsense, no trick to turn the attention inward without the world in its overwhelming entirety folding in upon itself. No way to rest, no will to resist the forward motion, the scheduled agenda and well-intentioned time line leading toward utter exhaustion.

Another month, another frightening flow of blood. What's left of the woman in me pouring out in grief. And my chest weighted and heavy, the act of breathing becoming a thing I must hold in my thoughts, like a step in a newly learned dance, a simple movement I must remind myself how and when to properly carry out.

So of course we plan another trip, the kids and I, to Delaware, to meet with the university professors who've conditionally approved my return to the doctoral program. It's a done deal, unless I screw up, and I have absolutely no intention of doing that. I pile everyone in the car and head south, ridiculously proud of myself for not making a single wrong turn or inappropriate lane change in the four-hour drive.

We stay with Ott's sister and her husband, in the spacious barn they've spent years lovingly renovating into a warm and comfortable home. Rich terra-cotta tile in the kitchen, exposed beams hung with harness leather, off-white walls and windows everywhere, summoning in the bright sun. Just across a swell of pines, fat and full as if groomed for Christmas, stands our own first home, the three-bedroom ranch where our children were born. During that long weekend, I never walk through those trees to see it.

This must be hard for you, she says.

Her gardens are end-of-summer beautiful, abundant late lilies blooming large and vivid tiger orange by the pool, reflecting globe low amid a bed of perennials, huge rosemary bush standing guard at the kitchen door. Like her brother, she's tall and sharp as they come, quick to laugh, with the same dark chocolate eyes and thick hair gone prematurely gray. Like the flowers in her garden, she keeps her sadness to herself. I crush a few spiny rosemary leaves between my fingers, bring them to my nose to smell.

It's not so bad, I say, grateful for all she and her husband have done for us. The visits to Connecticut to check on us, the calls on the sixth day of the month, when others have forgotten. *Ott isn't here.*

But I don't talk about the dreams. I don't say how when the house is dark and quiet, when everyone else is in bed, I pour another glass of wine and sit out on the stone steps and let the memories run free, memories that at daybreak I divorce.

In the morning I start the round of meetings at the university, first with the new director of graduate studies, a small, thin woman in whose seminar on Joyce, all those years ago, I'd hardly distinguished myself. She talks of the necessities, of money, of credit hours left to be earned, instructs me to be sure to follow up on this detail and that.

She's softer than I remember, she's kind to me, but still all business, and I think of a paper I wrote for her, another in a string of B or B minuses, near failure in graduate school, a paper in which she questioned my unschooled, undocumented comment on the abiding sadness of the Blessed Virgin Mary. *Why is Mary a sad figure?* she asked. I can still see her red remarks written in the margin. And I remember thinking then, after many years of devotion to the Holy Mother, who answered my prayers, who appeared in my dreams, how could you call yourself an Irish scholar, how could you call yourself a human being, and not understand the abiding sadness of the Blessed Virgin Mary?

And I meet, too, with a young Jewish studies professor who will advise me, and then the distinguished Nabokov scholar who will direct my dissertation, a beautiful woman, black hair perfectly coiffed, magnificent eyes enhanced with a dark line along the lash. She sets me at ease at once, she wants the best for me, I can tell, knows what I've been through, how I'm trying to move on. Together we agree on the course of study, and though an offhand comment she tosses my way goes right over my head, a remark on a novel at the top of the reading list I hold in my hand, a novel I thought I knew well, I leave feeling confident, and blessed, and privileged to be working with her.

The frenetically brilliant Byron scholar who's so smoothly engineered my return to academia takes me to lunch at the university's Blue and Gold Club. He's newly divorced or separated after a long marriage, and seems, good Catholic boy he might be, not particularly broken up about it. He's tall and attractive and altogether charming, in a teasing way that makes a body want to pinch him now and then. He once said a dress I was wearing made me look a little like an upholstered chair. Or was it a couch? A man has to have a way about him to say such things and be easily forgiven, and he has it. But he could do with a bit of feminine attention, I can see. The cuffs of his shirt are fraying and worn, and I imagine a new woman tossing that old rag, and him waking one morning to find a perfect replacement, pressed and ready, waiting in the closet. Some smart woman will see to that right quick, I predict, sipping a gin martini, my latest poison of choice. I know I should pay attention, not run wild on the significance of threads of a shirtsleeve. He's talking about *Frasier,* why he admires the writing, the clever dialogue, and I'm lost, I've no idea what writer he's talking about. I run through the canon of authors, American, English, modern, Victorian, draw a complete blank, and my face must tell him that, because then he says, "I mean the television show, Denise." And we laugh.

The Byron scholar will stay on the midlife dating market ten minutes at most.

And the work of the trip is over, well accomplished I feel, and I can relax. I see an old friend, buy myself a purple fringed shawl and a Ching dynasty footed bowl in an antique store, take the kids to visit my godmother down at the beach. She calls me *Doll,* feeds us all full of pasta. That last evening we're back with Ott's sister, sitting by the pool as the sun goes down, chilled wine in good glasses, the kids splashing in and out of the darkening water, laughing, playing chicken, showing off their best dives and most explosive cannonballs for their devoted aunt and uncle. Then the bugs come out, and then the bats follow, driving us inside for the night.

I dream of my husband again. He rises up from the bed of stone, wounded, changed. He's full of love for me, his eyes are wide and bright, he kisses me, takes me in a solid embrace. *Come with me!* he says, with the practicality of the dead and free, as if for a date, as if for an evening out. *Come with me!*

I whisper to him I can't, he knows I can't. He's not upset. He's happy to have seen me, in the dream. He loves me in the dream, his love fills the air around us, it's real as a sunrise, plain as the joy on his face.

And then he says, still clasping my hands tight, still smiling, looking into my eyes, *It'll be soon enough.*

We return home to find the neighbors upset over the barking dogs the house sitter was unable to quiet at night, and to face the untimely death of Ms. Tickles, one of the family guinea pigs, whom I'd instructed be wrapped in several layers of plastic bags and stowed in the garage freezer. Seemed like the thing to do at the time. There'll be a funeral, of course, a nod to sadness though not many tears shed at the shoebox burial in the tree-laden backyard. We've acquired a menagerie since we lost Ott—two dogs, two cats, and now the little pigs, smelly things I wish I'd said "no" to, and which the girls, their loving owners but squeamish caretakers, might have wished as well. In time will come fish and birds, much later another dog and cat. We're needy, longing for love, and we find it in small animals to cuddle against or cradle.

I put my foot down about the python, though, my son's request, the quiet young man in black, who has gathered that a mother's grief will readily loosen the restraints of parental good judgment and the drawstrings of her purse. "Dad said he'd buy me all the James Bond movies!" he announces one afternoon, glancing up from the screen across which the dashing and beautiful play at espionage, not the slightest hint of guile on his young face. His father's face.

I just look at him. By now it's become something of an old trick. "Don't do this to me."

He turns back to the tube. Worth a try.

This is the same child who, at three years old, mimicking a scene from television perhaps, pulled a dollar bill out of the pocket of his jeans, pressed it into my hand and said, "You've been a great mom. Keep up the good work." The same child who, sophomore in senior high, while I'm in agony over yet another abysmal report card, will explain to me in all sincerity, "I don't need good grades. I've got charisma."

And so we're unpacked and settled from the long weekend away, enmeshed in the routine of readying for school, of visits from the neighbors' children, of grocery runs and dirty socks scooped out from under the bed. And I am coughing up blood.

The doctor listens to the congestion in my lungs. *How long?* she asks. And I say, *A month, maybe two.*

Bronchitis, of course. I show her my finger, purple and swollen, cut recently on a cat-food tin. So a tetanus shot for that, and antibiotics for my lungs, a strong quick course that tortures my guts.

I know this won't do, merely tending the breakdowns of the body, minding the store on peak hours alone. It's not enough to see that a protein, a starch, and a green vegetable are served for supper, that lights in the children's rooms are out at a decent hour, that schedules for both work and play are adhered to like something out of Deuteronomy, that areas in the house on public view are kept tidy and clean. It looks good, it'll fool most everybody, but it simply won't do.

There's a six-week waiting list to see the psychiatrist the kind nurse at Hartford Hospital recommends. I can't wait six weeks. I don't have six weeks. I'm too embarrassed to return to the renowned white knight I'd seen just after Ott's death. I've fallen too low. I call a therapist in my town, and speak into a machine. When I set down the phone, I can't be sure I've left my number or even my name for him to reply.

He doesn't call back right away, and when he does, there's a lag of long days between the call and the appointment. The kids come home from their soccer practices with game schedules, and the physical impossibility of complying weighs me down like a lead apron—to be in two places at once, here with my son, there with the girls, the sheer exhausting anticipation of having to drive them all over hell and Connecticut, creation and back. I collapse in the hallway when they leave the house to play.

Can't you come home? I ask my dead husband, as if there's an answer he can send through the air, simple grounds to excuse these months gone by, a plane that's been missed, a consulting job that's overrun its target completion date. *Why can't you come home?*

And when I do manage, when I somehow pull it off, I feel like a genius, Madame Curie and Madeleine Albright rolled into one. Somehow I do muster the skills to point the car and myself and several small children dressed in assorted uniforms in a northerly direction, direct us again in another, and after deliberate and significant pauses at each location, reverse the route and travel home. And in the evening, I gussy up a bit for the kids' open house, if earrings and eye makeup can be said to constitute the necessary accessories of high fashion. I make the small talk, I confer with the teachers across low metal desks, I tell the good women friends I pass in the hall, *Yes, I'll call you, we'll meet for coffee.* Not much of an accomplishment, a single day of single parenthood, the petty problems and elementary logistics marginally surmounted, but it counts for something, I tell myself. It must. Leave tomorrow to tomorrow, as Jesus said, today has enough worries of its own.

When I cope, when for even a few moments I gather the world together like a ball of twine, I feel a peace, a beginning of it, the coming of a heartening change. The long summer is fading, and fall is rolling softly toward us; fall, with its rest and harvest and muted light. It's time to pot up the geraniums still blooming by the front door to winter over in the Florida room, time to plant masses of mums in their stead. Time to see at last the ordinary beauty I've overlooked all season, in flowers still holding on in my garden or the five-dollar bouquet in a hallway vase, in Latin music playing on the radio, in a sweet cherry tart baked for us alone. Peace. At night I let my mind drift before sleep. I visualize an ancient place of tall columns and white drapes flowing between them, a stone square open to the sun and warm breeze, a sanctuary set high on white cliffs, blue ocean waters far below. A place where I can go in my mind, whenever I need to, whenever I'm lost, a place where pain and worry rise up in the air like simple breath.

My therapist looks a little transplanted, like my beloved geraniums, a man who in another century, in a vastly different landscape, could have hewn a small forest and roped a herd of cattle without breaking a sweat. Tall and dark, bearded, no tie I recall, he holds himself apart a bit, in check, a studied demeanor no doubt necessary to the profession. Some poor woman patient has fallen in love with him, I trust, and he doesn't want to go through that headache again.

I tell the story. I tell him who I was and who I am now, I tell him I'm sick, that I drink too much and need to stop, that I can't do it on my own. I wander in my talk, ramble through the fifty minutes, letting anger out in sharp pieces, sadness in fits and starts. It's too late for halfway measures, too late for worries about my tearing mascara or whether the notes on the pad he holds in his large hands will end up in a permanent patient file.

And he listens, showing little reaction, little or nothing crossing his face in response. It's their way, I suppose, presenting a calm façade in hopes that it might be reflected back, or maybe he's heard it all before, in one anguished guise or another. He gives me homework as the session wanes, tells me to write down a list of "health-care goals" and how and when I stray from them. He suggests that maybe we should meet again, quickly, sooner than a week.

Because I've told him what I've told no one else, and rarely myself. I've told him, *All summer, I've wanted to be dead. All summer, I have longed for death.*

5

A Shower of Roses

T HE BOARDROOM, DEEP INSIDE THE PROTECTIVE WALLS AND HIGH-TECH security features of the new corporation headquarters, the carefully selected retreat taken up after that unfortunate day in March, where the distinguished members meet each month, reminds me of the observation deck aboard the *Starship Enterprise*. The dozen groomed and polished officials sit around the sleek console, which, like that on the show, curves up and about a raised platform, arcing at its midpoint, where I assume sits the silent chairman, commanding and photogenic as Captain Kirk himself. He has the best hair of the bunch.

I haven't trimmed or tended my own hair in six months. I've pulled it back, away from my face, uncharacteristically kempt and held in check with an old barrette, as if on purpose, as if I didn't just realize that very morning I looked a sight and had to do something. But none of that matters now. I am here, at the foldout table at the front of the room, before the board of directors at last, notes in my shaking hand. I've got something to say.

The acting president believes I've requested to speak to the board to support his claim to the throne. I do nothing to dispel this illusion, entirely wrongheaded as it is. He seems to me enormously well pleased with himself this afternoon, though on what account I haven't a clue. Perhaps he's imagined the impassioned speech I am about to give, the somber widow addressing the lords and barons of the realm, passing on the golden crown to the fallen leader's chosen successor. High drama, indeed, worthy of antiquated ceremony and weighty costumes, a scene right out of Shakespearean tragedy, or an early episode of *Star Trek*. But I am not here on behalf of anyone able to speak for himself.

The reporter I'd overheard in the lobby vociferously defending his right to attend the board meeting to a skeptical security guard has left the building. Had he opted to stay for the meeting's second half, I'd not have been allowed to speak, nor would I have wanted to. I've come to make a plea, not issue a public scolding. I settle in my seat, recognizing a few faces only. For the most part they're blank, the faces around the room, the faces of busy folks who need to be elsewhere, important leaders in business and government. I sense I ought to get on with things, I ought to hurry this along.

And I don't know how much of the speech I'd drafted in my journal I deliver, if I say that I'd heard of teachers throwing themselves in front of students in the line of fire, of teenagers downing armed assailants, that I live each day knowing corporation security did nothing for my husband, that the last vile words he heard still ring in my head. Did I say outright, as I have in my notes, that the police report was a waste of time, that only a thorough internal investigation could help prevent what happened from happening again?

I don't remember the words coming out of my mouth, I don't remember them echoing in the empty atmosphere above our heads. I don't know now if I was strong enough to say those things bluntly, without equivocation. Was I forceful and direct, or mousy, beaten, overwhelmed? I recall my hands and voice shaking. I recall a redheaded board member writing down everything I said, though now I cannot be sure what made it into the air.

But I know I tell them, loud and clear, that I need the board's help to understand what has happened, how to carry on in light of it. I need them to act. What is your moral response to mass murder? I ask. You have a spiritual burden, a responsibility. Mine is to my children; yours, I say, is not just to the corporation, but to those who are gone. That corporation was Ott's world, not mine, and I do not profess to know how it ought to be run. But it was the crown jewel in his career. It was his vision brought to light. I ask them not to simply remember him as they go on, but to respect him and all his good work, to honor him as they move forward, which is infinitely more difficult.

Before I leave, I speak again of the need to make sense of what has happened. For without that, I hear myself say, there's no reason to live.

I never receive an official response, or any response for that matter, from the board as a group or singularly. But the following day, the corporation's young attorney calls to tell me that they voted unanimously to double the amount in the trust funds set aside for the children's education. A fact that in the future will be brought to the attention of the press, whenever one of the family members of the March 6 dead gets out of line.

Forgive me, but even then, even though I thanked them and was grateful, it felt like money for blood and silence.

Oh, the close woman colleague of Ott's says at that dinner out, or perhaps later on the phone, when I talk of the board and how I heard nothing. *You wanted a response?*

My therapist is a man of action, not theory; he speaks out rarely and never minces words when he does. He tells me point-blank that I've been using alcohol to escape my feelings as well as my responsibilities. "Hold your own feet to the fire," he says, after I've gone on about the board, the impossibility of ever learning the whole truth about that morning in March, the inaction of those in positions to act. "Your children and your memories are what you have left."

It's not easy to have a stranger point out your failings, your weaknesses. I tell him I'm trying. I describe my daily lists of things to do for the house and the kids, lists long as your arm, and how I muddle through them, scratching items off one by one. I don't say how I feel I'm swimming in waters over my head, or how maybe I've already drowned. I talk about those lists, the accomplishment of getting through them, the satisfactions inherent in fourth-grade vocabulary drills and folded laundry.

"That's good," he says encouragingly, I can picture him still, long legs stretched out, arms crossed loosely, or one elbow edged against the desk, his body simply too big for the furniture. "It is. But, now—how about that list of things to do to take care of yourself?" Cut way back on the drinking, he says, and see how it feels. Pet the dog, take a walk, do something other than pour a glass of wine.

I hear myself say that I drink at night because I'm lonely, the house is quiet, there's nobody there.

"Your kids are there," he says sharply. And it's true, of course, and I'm horrified at what I've said. But then I think, they're in bed asleep no later than nine, and the rest of the evening is an empty sky.

"So call a friend," he says.

And with this, in front of him, I start to cry. I don't want to make those calls anymore, don't want anyone to realize how bad off I still am, to sense that misery on the line, to groan a little to themselves upon recognizing my voice. And truth be told, I don't know anyone who'd want to hear from me at nine in the evening.

You're more confused than ever, my friend from graduate school days has told me in our latest phone conversation, well-intentionally cutting me off midstream with the advice that I commit another list to paper, this time a daily schedule to follow like the ordinary of the Mass. She's tired of hearing about my life and would like the chance to gripe about her own. It's only fair, I know, it's what friends do for one another. But I'm not sympathetic to her troubles, I half listen, I tell her bluntly to quit the job she bemoans at length, to attend to the body that's wearing out before poor health breaks her in two. I don't realize it's not advice she wants but a chance to vent. She wants a friend. I've forgotten how to be one.

She stops calling for a while, like some others; what should a person expect, why should they bother, when I've no compassion for the ruined dinner parties and bungled haircuts of everyday life, when the talk of home remodeling and European getaways fails to elicit my resounding applause, when the complaints about a living husband's golf mania or inattention to housekeeping leave me cold. *He's alive,* I want to say, *he's there with you every night and at the breakfast table the next morning, at Fourth of July and Labor Day picnics, he fills the car with gas, and picks up pizza when it's late and there's nothing in the fridge, he remembers your birthday with flowers and an armful of gifts. What are you bitching to me for?*

So some friends fall away that autumn, my connections with the human race start to split and sever like cables holding a rusting bridge aloft. I am a profound disappointment to everyone I know.

What if now he's gone, I ask myself, *what if now, he's relieved to be free of me?*

We're at McDonald's, the kids and I, on a busy Saturday, just after noon, nothing in the house to eat and everyone is starved. The place is full of faces I don't recognize, it's packed, five deep waiting in the lines, tables surrounded with noisy teenagers, crews of workmen in odd-numbered groups, couples with young children climbing on seats and shouting.

We reach the register, my son standing before me, the girls already wandered off, one twin watching herself on the surveillance camera, the other I don't know where and it worries me. I tap my son's shoulder, hurry, hurry, hurry, let's get on with this. The clerk is a snooty teenager, she can't work the complicated buttons and it's our fault. I'm tapping harder, out of patience, and then I think, *What am I doing?* Everyone, I'm sure, is staring at me, watching me hit my son. "Did I hurt you?" I ask, and he looks at me blankly, wonders what I'm talking about. We pay and wait some more, gather drinks, straws, and napkins before finally sitting at a tiny table by the window, inches away from other tiny tables, all crowded with strangers.

We dole out the food, barely start to eat, when it hits me, the certain knowledge that we're being watched, that someone in the crowd has a gun, or someone just outside the door, someone ready to step through the glass and metal and raise the weapon to his shoulder, an automatic rifle most likely, the type that will do the most damage, that will kill the most with the least effort. It's not the men sitting right next to us, the greasy-looking assortment minding their own business, shoveling fries and thick burgers into their mouths, but they might be involved, they might be part of the plan, as could any of these people, this slovenly mob.

Trespassers will be shot.
Survivors will be shot again.

I'm too frightened to even look around, convinced the only thing to do is leave immediately, and I say, *Now, we have to go, right now, take what you want or throw it out, we can't stay another minute, now, now, now.* And I hustle out the kids like I've seen hens shelter chicks running before them under both wings, when I was a kid myself growing up on the farm, when something troubling, human or not, grew too near, and I do the same now, shuffling the children ahead of me and out, into the car, back home, where I close and lock the door.

In the grip of fear, it's hard to remember who you are, that you weren't always poised to run, that strangers aren't necessarily sinister, that a sudden noise might easily turn to song.

I think of when we were starting out, Ott and I, when we were new, dolled up for a night of dancing, down by the water on Maryland's eastern shore on a narrow dock as the sun was sinking into the bay. Steel drums, smiling men playing them, steady rhythm in the cooling air. The strap of my dress falling off one shoulder, my very best beau laughing as he turned and twisted about before me, all eyes in the small dinner crowd on the happy, attractive couple caring naught for anything but each other.

Who knows me now as I was then, young, sweet-tempered, the flush of life rising in my cheek, new love in my heart heady as the scent of a deep-red rose?

Well, no one, of course. No one at all.

The proper Connecticut authority to whom I've sent that pamphlet on assassination turns out to be a lovely, bright woman with an open mind and heart. "I was so happy to see your name on my call sheet," she says indulgently, phoning me again. I don't know how many times I've pestered her with this or that, and what in the world is she to do about it but listen, hindered as she is by the time-hardened restraints of bureaucracy, which in her nimble fashion she eventually bends. We make plans, we meet for lunch, at an Italian place I like, and I dress the part, it's been a while but I still remember how. And I recall her early words on the phone, *I hope this won't make you bitter. I hope you can be happy again.*

At our lunch, we don't talk so much of death, the supposed reason why we've met. We talk of love, of her second marriage to a man she adores, of growing children and blended families, of getting what you want and need. She's a smart woman, savvy and accomplished, and there's a kindness about her, genuine and rare, and I wish we'd met in different circumstances, I wish we could become good friends, I could do with a good woman friend, one I've not overwhelmed with the obligations of tragedy, one for whom I'm not a conversational wasteland, who would still find an hour's lunch with me a pleasure.

I tell her about my own children, my dreams, what I want, that I'm a writer, that I will write one day about all that has happened, but our talk turns back to men, how I should find one, how I should go out, have fun, I'm too young to sit at home alone. Pick someone, she says, maybe even someone married, it needn't be for love, it needn't be for life, just a good man who will treat me well, appreciate me, get me out of the sad rut, back into the world.

And you think about it, about finding a man, how can you be a woman, breathing, wanting, and not think of, not consider, your own joyless body in the mirror, your hair, your skin coarse and dull from the lack of simple touch, your mouth gone sour and dry. I look, I want, I watch the ones I like best, the well-built men with color in their cheeks, who love the outdoors and spend hours at a stretch in the sun, in the wind, men who look like they're good with their hands. I imagine, I dream. I'll say to the man, *whatever you do, for God's sake, don't ask me what's happened, don't bring it back to mind, don't speak at all unless to tell me a story, something cheerful, light as air, tell me news of a beautiful part of the world you've seen, or a joke so simple I'll get it straight off, nothing too clever, nothing demanding.*

And I do, of course, pick a man, a friend, and we go to lunch, men are easier over lunch than women, they want so very little. He wears a good dark suit and a crisp white shirt, he takes me to a far corner of the state, to an elegant restaurant, a tall, wide room of glass from floor to ceiling, and silver heavy on the table, extraordinary food, the best of wines. I drink all that I want, he's driving, I don't care, and I take him home, to the guest room, new linens on the bed, new comforter turned down, the kids out and tended by others, the house quiet. But I'm not there, I'm no good at all, the body moves like a cat in the dark, but the heart stays numb, it hardly beats, and then it's over, sponged down and dressed, done, done, done.

As a woman not yet dead, as one who once loved love for its own sake, I'm a little ashamed to say how long I wait before I try again.

I phone a good friend and say I've gone out to lunch with a man, just lunch, that's all I tell her. That's enough. This development concerns her greatly, she has my very best interests at heart when she speaks. *I'm going to talk to you like a big sister,* she begins, and she warns of the gossip likely to follow such a foolhardy thing as going out to lunch with a member of the opposite sex, that my neighbors are surely watching at their picture windows, will note the comings and goings of strange cars, will calculate the minutes they remain parked in the driveway and will wonder over coffee with other neighbors about what sort of things might be taking place inside the house during that time. I need to be aware of this, my friend says. People will talk, and that talk will be cruel.

I'm astonished. I had no idea I might be a creature of such community fascination. I've been an ordinary little dumpling my whole life, and now that tragedy has found me, I'm something of a femme fatale.

I thank my friend, of course, one thanks one's friends for pointing out the idiocies in one's life, but as I hang up the phone I think, *Dear Jesus! I need many things these days, but I don't believe a "big sister" is one of them.*

I'm wrong, of course. I need all the help I can get.

The Hubble telescope radios back new views from space, an explosive cosmography, a luminous spiral galaxy with its tentacles wrapped tight, and an eye of bright yellow, like the yolk of an egg, they say, fertile as well, for around its hazy edge stars themselves are coming into being. Or they were, once, long ago, as the light we see was sent on its way billions of years before. What do I know of time and space, then or now, watching the news and falling into these vibrant images like a traveler in a trance, or years later, living under the wide northern sky? Almost nothing at all. That I've wished upon the first dot on the far horizon since I was small. That I've spent chilly nights under heavens hazy and clear, watching meteor showers with my first-born girl, who thinks she might be an astronaut one day. That her father let his mind wander into the night when he couldn't sleep, let himself imagine he was shooting headlong among the stars.

A massive star in our own galaxy blooms like a jungle flower, or an iridescent globe blown from hot glass. In the reflection lies the past. I think of a theory I read in a book as a child, of time folding back upon itself like a wrinkle, joining what was then with what is now, or perhaps even what will be. I think of lives spent in parallel, one existence fulfilling the failed desires of another, the end of breath in one, a new beginning in the next. I crave but I can't fathom it, I want to believe, I want reassurance certain as the rising sun. I look instead on photographs from a telescope floating in space, burning gases expanding against the black, the lovely charred remains. Maybe some yet undiscovered science, or magic, or both, will bring the edges of the universe together for us at last. *Reunion is sweet,* he said to me in a dream. But I'm only flesh, I can't cross that gulf. How can the light from a human heart span the darkness of a billion years?

About this time I learn, or I finally do the math from figures at the ready, that my husband and the others have been slaughtered for a discrepancy in pay amounting to roughly $2,000.

Rage. I fear becoming a caricature of rage, that madwoman in the torn sweater filling out the mob scene in the bloody foreign film, the screaming psycho on the bridge. I worry that the thinnest thread keeps me tied to the world of the sane. I tell my therapist, toward the end of another largely feigned hour of calmness, before I gather my purse and go, that the anger overwhelms me, that I can't sleep, that I'm afraid of everything, of strangers in the supermarket, of sinkholes in the backyard, of the ringing phone in the middle of the day. I tell him, "I want to get a gun and shoot things."

A hint of unease crosses his customarily impassive face. "It concerns me to hear you say that," he comments soberly. As well it ought to have, one supposes.

I'm amazed at what's come out of my mouth, and assure him I'd never do such a thing, I'd never hurt anyone. I couldn't.

He nods, he knows of course I wouldn't. But in the next breath, for the first time he offers drugs to help me sleep, to calm me down.

When the New York job fell through a lifetime ago, when Ott drove home from New York City to Delaware in the gray boat of a company car someone else would sail away, and we began those long months of uncertainty, the year of tailored résumés on pale ocher vellum and austere shopping lists crafted with equal care, my godmother sent me a laminated devotion to Saint Therese, the saint they call the Little Flower, patron to pilots, orphans, and the dying, who no doubt hears the pleas of children and fools as well. Who answers prayers sent her way with roses.

I write in my journal, apropos of nothing in the surrounding entries—remarks on a dream faintly recalled, on a heartening lunch with a friend for which I'm grateful, and a wish that I'd been a better wife—that Saint Therese answers prayers with a rose.

What prayers I've asked her to answer, why I've remembered Saint Therese at all just now, I cannot say.

I dream of flowers surrounding the house, exotic blooms on thick jungle stalks, birds of paradise, red ginger, anthurium, all growing wild in suburban Connecticut, the flowers I chose to decorate the altar for the funeral mass, the ones paid for by the corporation.

I dream of an attractive woman all in black, with dark hair and a pretty smile, trying to lead a normal life though there's a huge black flower in the middle of her face, where her nose ought to be, this strange black flower. Everyone can see the flower, everyone knows why it's there, but she carries on despite the stares, the ignominy, she even rises from her seat to dance when asked, she knows she must go on. When I speak to the woman, when I greet her kindly, her eyes turn down, she's ashamed. But I think to myself she must be very brave.

My research toward a doctorate in English literature takes on a behemoth life of its own, stretches out into a psychic minefield, some charged space between migraine and nightmare. I gather the materials, the books, the dozen photocopied articles all highlighted in fluorescent yellow and pink, my neatly penned three-by-five-inch file cards, and strew it all out on the guest bed, as if by chance the pieces will fall into some sensible order, proclaim some divinatory relevance I've failed to extract. The scholarly works have little relation to the masterpieces they aim to critique; they are so dense and dull you need a machete to hack your way through the prose and a bullshit barometer to assess what's left standing. Intellectually pretentious, laden with references to long dead and rightly obscure linguists, the collection of academic crap reminds me of the ease with which I abandoned the course of study with the birth of my girls, like the loss of a rotting molar way in the back of your mouth, an ache you'll never miss.

I want to write a beautiful book! I note in my journal, along with my frustration, and the growing certainty that I'm already a failure. *A beautiful book!* Camille Paglia, who writes of literature like a dream, in terms of beauty and decadence, who speaks to fundamentals, to sex and death, to Nature and Man, is my hero in exegesis.

I'm no Camille Paglia, but I carry on, nonetheless. I've purchased two cheaply bound photocopied dissertations on subjects similar to my own, and

I study them like geometry, so I know what's expected in this sample chapter I'm writing, so I have a formula of what makes for the appropriate height and width and depth of literary inquiry. I revise and revise the thing, reconsider its organization, pull it apart and Scotch tape it back together until eventually it's as vapid and verbosely vague as the most highly esteemed critical pieces I've studied.

I'm not a failure! I tell myself. *I can obfuscate with the best of them!* I will succeed, I will a make a life for myself and the kids, I won't be forever beholden to the financial whims of the state of Connecticut.

Thirty pages of practically unreadable fine print, I believe, hold my very future.

I will worry about money for the rest of my life.

It's late in March, years later. I'm driving my son home from school, reviewing his academic day as we always do. Only, on this afternoon we're cheerful, the report is improving, and as if in celebration, the long months of snow have nearly disappeared. A few scruffy ridges of sooty white remain along the roadsides. Every spring I fall in love with dirt.

But this winter's been insanely long and hard, the coldest in nearly a quarter century, the temperature falling well below zero for too many days at a stretch. The old house has garnered a few more creaks and cracks, and quite frankly, so have I. I say to my son, sitting next to me in the passenger's seat, tuning into a techno song on the radio, "Wouldn't it be wonderful to have a townhouse somewhere warm, Key West, Savannah? To escape the cold for a while?"

And he says to me, the mother he holds dear to his heart, the woman he turns to for comfort and love: "How will you afford it, Mom? You're too old to strip."

Another midweek soccer match for the girls, way up near the Massachusetts border, a gray late October day, though not without its charm. The air is brisk and damp from a rain not long fallen; a sweater feels good against the skin, pulled up high on the back of the neck. We're at a field nestled in behind some houses, a line of trees on the other side, a lovely spot. The coach of the opposing team is a hotheaded windbag, though, snapping at his players, berating the ref, challenging something, it seems, every time the whistle blows. His shrill squawk carries from the center line, slapping the air while the beautiful mother of another young soccer star introduces herself. She must be a model, or have been, I think; she's nearly six feet tall and blessed with the fair, all-American good looks seven scores of merchandisers would kill to have in their advertising corner. But there's not a trace of vanity in her talk or manner, or makeup on her exquisite face. She's married to one of our team's two coaches, a very handsome man himself. They've just returned, she tells me, from an anniversary trip to Italy.

Italy, I say. *How wonderful! I've always wanted to go.*

The game is nearing the end, another sure victory for our girls. Defeat is uncommon, and I suspect in many households not well-tolerated. You sense in these families, the Yuppie couples dressed in J. Crew, pulling out matching folding field chairs from L. L. Bean from late model Volvo wagons, a competitive spirit being passed from parent to child, tactics barely needing translation from the boardroom to the playing field. Run fast. Kick hard. Guard your goal. Cut ahead of your opponent. Trip them when necessary. Win, win, win.

A man and a woman emerge from one of the homes behind us, their voices rising in the chilly air. "This is not public property!" they say. "This is *town* property. You can't hold a game here!" They shout at the coaches and walk right onto the field, ending the match, the young girls in their damp, pale blue uniforms standing about nervously at first then dispersing to the sidelines. The hotheaded coach goes at the pair, the decibels rise, their voices growing uglier and more frightening, a little circle forming, an angry stupid mob.

And I can't help it, it comes to me in a flash, like the silent glow at the far horizon that precedes a stormy night, I think, *What if one of them has a gun?* And in the grip of that foreboding, I gather up my girls like china dolls; gesturing quick and mindful as the dumb, I grab their gear, their bags, and their drink bottles, and without good-byes or explanation, hurry them into the car and drive away.

That fall fear keeps me in its crosshairs, keeps me up against the wall, paralyzed in its glare. Fear of failing my children, of failing my heroic husband. Fear of both the familiar and the strange, of the past and the hazy future, of pain itself, of amounting to nothing at the end of a miserable, wasted life. I write my daily lists of things to do as a hedge against chaos, a means to gather some control. Lists of ways to keep my children happy, healthy, thriving and safe; lists of ways I am sure Ott would want me to conduct myself; lists of cages to rattle in the state of Connecticut to address my husband's death. Lists by which I somehow hope to feel secure.

And I pray. I pray, I pray, I pray.

It almost works, it almost succeeds, this strategy—half sacred stunt, half self-help mumbo jumbo. Except at night when the dreams come, when whatever meager grip I held on the day is lost and a troubled subconscious takes the reins. Dreams of the four dead found in dried out graves in the clay basement of an abandoned house. Dreams of my son lying ruined on the bed of stone with his father. Dreams of crawling onto the funeral pyre as my husband's body burns. Of churning oceans, and of splintered ships going down.

What good would it do to say, years now gone by, that driving on a dark road alone sometimes is altogether too much, or that two men standing at the back end of a pickup, stopping a conversation and raising their eyes to mine can unnerve me? That now and then hearing my footsteps echo in the alcove of an empty stair, the weight of something that day left undone, bills paid late, clothes forgotten in the wash, milk jug down to its last drop, the clutch of self-doubt and despair like a hand around my heart, that voice returns, the voice from that black first year. *She couldn't take it, you know, that woman, you remember her, that one, she couldn't stand another moment, she did it, finally, she did herself in.* Only now, I understand, by the time my feet touch the solid floor and my hand lets go of the banister, that it's nothing more than a voice from the past, the lulling song from the drowning woman I was, an echo I can choose to follow or not.

At some point after a great tragedy, I can't say exactly how or when, you realize all you thought you knew about your place in the vast, essential emptiness that is our universe is unfounded. Your importance, or your lack of it, your identity, your desires—all require a thorough review. Your vision shifts its limited perspective, you see now and then from high and low, and if you're honest in the act, are both humbled and emboldened.

You are reminded when things get too tedious or even too wonderful, when you take your strength for granted or your accomplishments too seriously, that if you have a modest place at the banquet table in this world at all, it's very likely because someone else equally deserving lost their reservation, or their nerve.

Ladies' night out after a long day. I fuss with my hair and makeup until I look more or less acceptable for a widowed woman approaching middle age. The sweet-faced sitter arrives, my three friends pull up in the driveway and off we go to Hartford, to a comedy club for dinner and a few laughs. The moon is huge, just past full, a "beaver moon" I think I've heard the meteorologist report. It follows us on our way.

I've had a glass of wine already. My spirits were low all afternoon; they begin to rise. The city seems pretty to me, washed clean by the chill in the air. Tall, illuminated buildings, small, square houses set close to the roadway. Looking into windows, curtains pulled aside, looking into people's lives. A man hoses down a ramp leading into a garage. Cars stop at a six-lane inter-section before speeding on. The sky darkens; the lights of the capital en-trance me, like holiday decorations holding a kid in a giddy spell.

The club is crowded with young people, long tables full of good-looking men and women in their early twenties, smiling constantly at one another, bringing steins of beer to their lips. "Families welcome!" a sign at the door had read, though I think not on this evening with its suspect entertainment, and think too that I've had enough of my family for one day. And I bet the other ladies have as well. We are happy with our mediocre meals, with the few hours of respite from homework checks and child hair-washes, from tables to clear and leftovers to cover with economy plastic wrap.

The first two comics are as mediocre as the food. A poorly dressed woman takes the microphone and, in the middle of a lackluster perfor-mance, tosses out an unflattering remark about the age of one of my friends, who has the bad fortune of sitting close to the stage and so is ready prey. It turns the mood uneasy, a violation of the camaraderie we'd found around our small, sheltered table. The next comic is an attractive man, not particu-larly funny, but I don't care. I like the way he looks, I daydream about having a man of my own.

The final act is worth the wait—an ugly fellow with a rubber face, perfect timing and a filthy mouth. Nothing in his world is sacred, his love life espe-cially, and by the end I've laughed so steady and hard, my insides feel like they've had a workout. We pile into the suburban mom minivan, and see the comic tossing his stuff into the back of a car parked on the street. "Roll down the window!" I say. "Tell him he was great!" We applaud and cheer, a huge smile cracks his wonderfully silly face in two.

I'm dropped off first. Hugs all around. The sitter is well paid and her older sister retrieves her promptly. The kids are sleeping dreamlessly, the house is completely quiet, and I feel, again, suddenly, intensely alone.

I pour a little more wine, rationalizing I've not had that much over the course of the long evening, and stand in the kitchen and think. And night of comedy or not, out it comes, the anger at heart, still fueling the end of a long day. *What kind of God allows mass murders to occur?* I ask. And then that re-frain, that wretched song, *Why is he dead, why is he dead, why is he dead?* I'm beating the counter with my fist, again and again, as if this will do some good, as if I'm beating the breath out of the lousy universe itself. I throw the glass against the wall and put on a coat, step out into the cold night.

The huge moon is now just a nickel. The dark air holds a few sparse stars, as if a miserly hand has rationed them out. I blame this on Connecticut. It's a pathetic Connecticut sky, I think. Nothing is good or beautiful in this state, this sleeping state, as asleep as the God who floats about us in the miserable empty night, the God who watches over us as if we were smelly renters in a crowded boardinghouse, taking in his weekly fee, fixing the plumbing when enough of us complain, but otherwise letting us rot. I sit on the stone wall my husband had built and sob.

In the morning my left hand is an exquisite display of bruising, green as moss along the edge of the palm and back around, the swollen knuckles crimson and purple. I can't understand why it only hurts when touched.

"I threw a wine glass against the wall," I tell the friend who'd been dissed about her age, who's called to see how I enjoyed the night. "I had a little fit, I guess."

And she says, "Well, I've done that, too! Was it red or white? Leave a stain? Felt good, I bet."

"You know," I say, "it did."

Even God seems to have forgiven me by the morning. My mind is clear, my heart is peaceful. God knows a sad, lonely rant when He hears one. I don't think He takes such a thing all that personally.

The work on the doctoral chapter has reached a point where if I redpencil the thing one more time, it will self-combust. Simultaneously appalled and proud, knowing that it's a bit of a one-noter and a little shallow, though heartened by comparison with the other dissertations, which are equally one-dimensional, I submit it to a final spell check in preparation to post it to the elegant Nabokov scholar. And, of course, the piece-of-junk printer won't work, dies on the very day of reckoning itself. I send the paper via e-mail to a friend and confidant who prints it out for me on excellent stock, reading it over as he does, giving me an enthusiastic thumbs-up. I see mistakes when he delivers it, but it's too late for changes now.

Off it goes, then, my footnoted and bibliographied future, held secure with a steel paper clip, a tidy bundle in a plain manila envelope.

It's the middle of November. I'm very tired.

In a few weeks, my husband's birthday will arrive. Just before then, Thanksgiving, and an anticipated visit from my brother and his family. How will we get through these "celebrations" without emotional collapse? How can we carve the turkey and pour the wine, give thanks for what we have while remembering too clearly what we have lost?

Some afternoons I take a vacation from these worries and haunt antique stores. There are many nestled about the area; many customers with the means to afford nice things. I'm one of them, I remind myself, though to a lesser extent. My parents, antique dealers themselves, first as a hobby and now their livelihood in their hard-earned retirement, have instilled in me an appreciation for quality, for fine workmanship acquired at a reasonable cost, for the very hunt for these things, the pleasure in discovering a small masterpiece of china or silver among the junk and debris in a merchant's dust-laden drawer.

North of the town in which we live sits another exclusive enclave, smaller, more village than suburb, where my family had briefly settled when I was a small child. My father was in insurance, he was a man with authority and responsibility in a national company, but increasingly small stomach for the cutthroat business practices. He bounced from position to position until finally leaving the industry altogether to take a teaching job in lower Delaware. But for a short while we lived in this bucolic corner of the state of Connecticut. I remember sliding on the icy road near our dark ranch home with its beautiful stone fence. I remember my mother chasing a frightened mouse out of the house with a broom, just as I would years later, my own kids tagging after me, fascinated, caught up in the pursuit. Only our mouse, instead of escaping through an open screen door, would commit hara-kiri by somehow jumping into the toilet.

On this shopping excursion, to a discriminating antique store in that little town of my childhood, I find a lovely set of Rose Medallion china. Not the very finest, the mid-nineteenth-century work that goes for thousands, but still beautiful, highly collectible, most of the pieces over a century old, the porcelain bowls paper-thin, the delicate hand painting in muted sea-greens and rosy pinks. I've collected this china for a while now, I know how to tell the superior pieces from the reproduction junk, and this is quality, this is what I crave. I lift the bowls up to the light, the outlines of my fingers shadows against the glow. It's a large set, nearly a dozen each of dinner plates and smaller ones as well, and fragile bowls, some of them with hairline cracks. A good price, one my parents would approve, and I tell the proprietess I'll take them, though I forgo the additional cups and saucers, a miserly mistake I will come to regret.

When I unwrap the loot on my dining-room table and arrange the plates and bowls in my china cabinet, I come to feel I was meant to find and have these lovely things. That this set, this small treasure, would bring me a little delight and stay in our family for years.

That night I dream of a bunch of young thugs breaking into the house. They terrorize me, taunting and laughing, running from room-to-room, shouting out, breaking things. They're here to rob us, to hurt us, and I'm paralyzed with dread. I can't get rid of them, I can't do anything at all. Finally, they take what they want and leave. I grab hold of one daughter by the hand and run outside; her brother and sister are nearby, my mother waits in the car next to the house. I know the thieves have turned on the gas and that the house will soon explode. I pull my mother from the car and we all run, away from the blast and flames.

I sit up straight in bed, snapping to attention but not afraid. It was only a dream. In the semidarkness of the bedroom, something hangs in the air before my eyes. Just hangs there, shapeless, like a mist. I even try to touch it, it seems so real, but my hand goes through it. I smile but can't make it out, and lay my head back on the pillow. The image moves with me, stays in my field of vision, and as I watch it turns into a rose in bloom, a deep pink, a flower of perfection. Suddenly the space around me fills with roses opening up, like smiling children turning their faces to the sun.

Then the whole room is full of roses, a sea of roses floating on the air, blossoms large as your outspread hand, until the blooms gently explode around me like shooting stars, a shower of vibrant pink, touches of gold in the charged air as the tear-shaped petals twist and fall.

And I remember the promise of Saint Therese, the patron known as the Little Flower of Lisieux: *I will let fall from heaven a shower of roses.*

On Ott's birthday, our daughters are dancing and playing with a friend. Our son watches a television show on computers, then takes the dogs for a walk. He is popular with the neighbors, they usher him into their homes, treat him to smiles and small gifts. I polish my mother-in-law's tea set, which I've allowed to tarnish so deeply the girls thought it was gold. After an hour of rubbing, it's restored, though a few stubborn spots remain.

I want lobster for our dinner. I want elegance and decorum. At the grocery store, though, the kids have other plans. They yank at me like a dishcloth hung on the fridge handle. They push my buttons until I'm utterly fried. One daughter sobs because she wants the expensive ice cream in the tiny decorated tubs. She won't let her brother hold the lobsters. He doesn't want lobster anyway, he says; he wants pizza instead, and twirls about like a sulking spastic when I won't buy it. My other girl concurs, no lobster for her, she wants tacos, and with meat, not just beans the way I sometimes make them, and candy too, and whines and stamps her foot when I pass by the half-aisle-long display of sweets.

I'm crying by the time I pay the cashier, a sensitive kid with thick dark hair, Beaver Cleaver smile, and soulful eyes. He looks about twelve himself. "They're a handful today, aren't they, ma'am?" he says.

Yeah, I needed the "ma'am." You bet.

By that evening, we are calm. I set the table with my new china, crisp linen beneath, and delicate flutes for each of us, into which I pour a thimbleful of Asti Spumante for the children and drop in a sugar cube to make the bubbles rise. We toast the one who is missing, the one we love and wish were with us still. The lobster is sweet; I've set out little bowls of salty, melted butter for dipping. The kids enjoy the crack of the shells, the informality of wet, crumpled napkins, the sheer mess of it all a blessing against the gravity of the day.

And after, I spend a full hour at the sink, carefully lathering those delicate plates, rinsing clean the soap from the hand-painted designs, the men and women in their glamorous, belted robes, the full-blown roses in shaded sweeps of mauve. I'm grateful for that hour, for that diversion, and it occurs to me in a way it never had before why perhaps the material thing has such power, why we long to possess not just the moment of passion rendered on the Grecian urn, but the Grecian urn itself. To hold a thing in your hands, to look at it with your own eyes, to distract your mind from what is gone with a piece of beauty that remains—there is a reason God made the rose so sweet.

6

Finding a Voice

A LETTER COMES HOME FROM SCHOOL. MY SON CAN'T SEE THE BOARD, HE can't make out the teacher's legible script, he needs his dark eyes examined right away. I pull him out of classes for this, I make an afternoon of it, a respite, a game. I'm pleased when the optometrist compliments his maturity and winning personality, when the technician who fits him with new glasses tells him someone—who must be me, who must be his mother—must love him very much to give him such a thing as wonderful as the electronic game he carries. My son smiles, he never refuses an opportunity to talk of games and computers. He responds to the praise, to the attention. And afterward, I take him shopping. We spend money on clothes and toys. More distractions.

Other mothers know that school is important. Other mothers would have scheduled this unavoidable affair for after-hours, for the rush between dismissal and dinner or lacrosse practice. Not me. An eye appointment has become an event, a celebration, a welcome break from the tedium of the day-to-day, recorded in red on the calendar and anticipated as a holiday. I'm a little in denial, a woman grasping a life-line, or maybe the string attached to a big red balloon. I don't fully comprehend when his teacher phones to tell me my son continues to do poorly in English, that he needs a constant push and prod, that his handwriting is hesitant. I don't want to hear that some days he's friendly, outgoing, talkative, that he's better than the opening weeks of the school year, when he sat alone, when he spoke to virtually no one, but there are days when he is plainly miserable. I don't want to believe that—my son, miserable.

I want, as any mother wants, her child simply happy. I want him rescued, whole and safe. I want him lifted up, scooped out of rough seas, settled on a wide span of sandy beach, every desire within an arm's length of a comfortable chaise lounge. I spoil him. I try to give him *unconditional love.* I've read somewhere that sons especially need that from their mothers, and I try to give it as I can, as best I understand it. I don't care if he prints his letters instead of linking into flowing script, or if he eats too many sweets before dinner, or spends too many hours chasing electronic monsters across a grainy computer screen. He is my son.

I write in my journal, *Hitler's father died when he was twelve. His mother doted on him.*

I know indulging him is bad parenting, I know if I persist, I'll turn him into a monster. But of the three children, his sadness is most clearly defined and frightening, perhaps because it is like my own. Maybe because he looks like his father, I cater to him, instead. Maybe because the girls have each other, on some intuitive level I feel they need me less.

I'm wrong, of course, as I will be wrong again and again, mothering my children. But something even then must have assured me, something about what had been wrought in them at conception, what together Ott and I had brought out before he was gone. Something that even a year or two of truly atrocious parenting couldn't undo.

One night, when my son was still very small, the baby girls were quiet in their cribs, and Ott was traveling, or maybe in New York, I heard some crying, some unintelligible toddler's talk in the dark. As I came awake, I heard another voice too, unfamiliar, unwelcome, muffled but decidedly masculine. And then nothing.

I snapped out of bed, my heart racing, stood still for a moment, then opened wider the door to our room. We were living in the ranch in Delaware, three bedrooms at the end of a short hall that led into the foyer and a great room. I stepped into the bright hall, under the overhead light I always kept burning, saw nothing, heard nothing, then checked on my son, unsettled in his sleep, tossing about middream, moaning out in sleepy mumbles. I touched his forehead, pulled at his summer covers. And then I heard the strange voice again, deep though seemingly distant, issuing what seemed a short, sharp command.

The breath rushed out of me, as if I'd been slapped.

Inside of me something surged, something came entirely alive. My body tensed, my senses shifted into highest gear. I could feel my eyes bulging in their sockets, my face muscles tightening, as I bounded for the bedroom door and grabbed the only weapon at the ready, the handle of a plastic toy I lifted high over my head. And I stepped back into the hallway, staring into the dark ahead of me, and shouted, in a voice I never knew I owned, "Who is it? Who's there? Get out! Get out of my house! Get out *now!*" I stood. I was shaking from toes to nose, a steady grip on that handle, and such resolve, ready to kill whoever might be bold enough to step near my children's bedrooms.

Then nothing. Quiet. My heart hammered like some factory piston, my breath came in heaves. But the house was entirely quiet. I turned to see my son, sitting curled up against his pillows, still a little too drowsy to be fully afraid.

Then we heard the voice again. The imagined intruder's ominous instruction to his henchmen waiting in the dark. And this time I recognized it. I knew immediately. I put down the toy in my hand, a child's play vacuum, the sort that bounces little plastic balls against a large hollow bubble when stroked across a carpet, and I opened my son's closet door. On the floor rested the latest mechanical acquisition, a voice-activated headset I'd bought for him, to teach vocabulary and a love of language, to play games with words and rhyme. The source of my nighttime terror. I examined it, shaking my head in self-disgust. I whispered *Hello!* into the microphone. The sinister monotone spoke again.

I showed it to my son. "Silly Mommy, huh?" He looked up at me in the quasi-dark, and I reshuffled his little self back into a proper sleeping position. Pillows and sheets adjusted, I let out a big, stupid sigh. "Silly Mommy." But I checked the locks on the doors and windows anyway, surveyed what could be seen of the property through the safety of glass, before heading back to my own room. Just to be on the safe side.

That first winter my husband is gone, I dream of a gentle hillside, a rippling sea of lush green grass, bloodred tulips lining the horizon as far as the eye can follow. An empty stretch against a vivid blue sky. Someone or something ought to be standing in the center.

The families of those lost in the March 6 slaughter are invited to a reception of sorts, hosted by the secretary of the state. The year's *Connecticut State Register and Manual* has been dedicated to those who died that day, I'm told, and a ceremony in their honor has been scheduled in Hartford. It's about time, I think. Someone ought to remember them. A good friend, a strong-willed, blue-eyed blonde from Puerto Rico, mother of four confident and beautiful girls, accompanies me, shares lunch in a favorite Italian restaurant, taxies me downtown. I'm wearing a size-four suit that is too big for me. I'm grateful she doesn't mention how hideous I look.

We're directed up a flight or two of steps to a small, square room full of folding chairs, a simple podium at one windowless wall. There might be a table of food or drink, or both, along another. Others from the corporation nightmare are gathered, the good-looking widower in an expensive suit, his hair gone noticeably gray; a fellow widow, much younger than I, who has brought her small children and a man—a boyfriend, I think—in an act I find both brave and likely foolhardy. Doesn't she have a "big sister," I wonder, to tell her what she ought and ought not do?

The room is full of people, strangers almost all, and we take our seats, my good friend next to me, as the presentation begins. With the conclusion of the opening remarks and pleasantries, I learn all about Abraham Ribicoff, Connecticut public servant par excellence, who held nearly every elective office and position of merit possible. I don't think I'd ever heard of him before. I know his name now. The book has been dedicated to his memory as well, to his unique and inspiring legacy. His family is grateful.

And then the talk turns to those we lost, a few minutes of airtime given our loved ones. A few heartfelt sentences on the sadness of March 6.

But the ceremony is not over. The *Register* is also dedicated to the theme "Connecticut Diversity." What follows and completes the day is a mélange of short speeches by politicos, self-congratulations from representatives of various commissions—the Latinos; the gays, lesbians, and bisexuals, whose leader thanks her partner; the African Americans; the elderly. The occasion devolves into a backslapping political lovefest, an opportunity to solidify a voting block, perhaps, to put in a good word for a grant or appointment, and I'm a jittery, squirming, pissed-off mess through most of it.

In honoring everyone, the state honors no one, of course. It's a nonevent, a photo-op, a zero. A poor television camera man, just doing his job, filming the low-budget festivities, receives my blackest stare.

So I go home and write another letter voicing my dismay. This time I write to an editor of the Hartford paper, about exactly what I cannot be sure. It hardly matters. No one is listening. A shrew is fairly easily ignored.

I decide to inform the acting president of the corporation about this letter. I get him on the phone, I think I'm doing him a courtesy, letting him know what I'm up to, what might appear in print.

He's not particularly grateful. He's had it with me already, he's tired of my calls, tired of my complaints. He's a good man, his wife is a good woman, they're caring and thoughtful, they've been kind to me, brought me mums for my autumn garden, come to the house and held my hand when I was despondent, when I needed comforting. That ought to be enough, I can tell by his voice. He doesn't want to hear about letters to the editor after he's put in a full day's work and lived up to his duty to me. He wants to be thanked for what he's already done.

But I see only the work that remains. I want more. Somehow, the subject turns to that red-bound police report. How little was revealed in it, how little was learned. And the acting chair tells me he never read it. "Was it sent to me?" he asks. I can't comprehend how he could not have insisted upon having it sent.

Had he questioned the man in charge of security, I ask, questioned the head of human resources? Had he discussed what happened that day, what led up to it, become fully informed as anyone in charge should have? Had he found out what he could and learned from it?

There's a pause, a catching of the breath before the blast. "What good would that have done?" he barks at me. "I was in enough pain."

Oh, yes, pain. I'm familiar with it, I know it well. But pain doesn't set aside our responsibilities. I'm stunned at the admission, that even this man who'd known us for over a decade did nothing. And I say, blurting it out, the weight of the wall I had thrown myself against all this time finally bearing down, "But he was your friend! He was your friend."

The voice on the line grows colder still, sharper. "What are you accusing me of?"

I answer simply, "Of not doing your job, I guess."

"Well, I guess I miss the point," is his reply.

The conversation is futile; the ramifications do not escape me. This mindset was one he shared with others, no doubt, ingrained, pervasive; five people were dead, and everyone in the corporation had missed the fucking point.

"Yes," I say. "I believe you have." I can remember my voice in reply, the quiet calm of it, the resignation, but with it, an understanding that this man had perhaps done the best he could, given who he was and what he feared. *You can't get blood from a turnip,* my mother used to say. That comes to me now. And there's no reason to continue. I tell this friend, the acting president, good-bye.

It was this conversation that ended the hopeful fiasco, that ended the fruitless round of fight, the faith that some good might still be found in a great and senseless loss. This conversation made up my mind. With it, I washed my hands clean of the corporation, of the state of Connecticut.

What did I want from him, what would have satisfied me, bitter, resentful widow I had become by then? What could he have done?

Nothing, I suppose, at that late date, nothing the lawyers would not have stopped him from doing. By this time, except for one of the March widows who still believed in the goodness of humanity, we were all lawyered up to our necks. At last count, some eighteen attorneys are engaged in this suit. A

small forest has given its life toward the endless documentation and court fil-
ings, to cc's to this office and that, to redundant notarized statements. Seven
years later, literally nothing has been resolved.

What did I want?

There was a time, God help me, when I wanted blood for blood. That
time, that anger and its unequivocal expression, had passed. But the pain
that lingered on wanted something significant in its place.

I wanted a thorough review. I wanted my husband's death in a mass
murder to receive a complete, exhaustive, internal investigation, one that
would determine what went wrong, as something *surely* did, to not have it
dismissed with a respectful, somber nod but still out of hand, as if it had
been a tragic act of God or nature, as if these poor souls had all suffered si-
multaneous heart attacks for which there was no forewarning.

I wanted peace of mind, a sense that his death had not been in vain.

I wanted clarity. I wanted the truth.

I wanted my husband back.

No one, of course, could give me that.

It would be incorrect to leave the impression that nothing at all was done
in response to mass murder. The state of Connecticut did significantly
tighten building security, and also instituted something called a Zero Tolerance Policy, which essentially states that if any employee performs the water-
cooler equivalent of holding up a sign saying he's about to kill someone, he
will be dealt with severely and in a timely fashion.

There are a few problems with both of these policies. The first is, the in-
dications of impending danger are not always so unsubtle and conducted as
well in the presence of those with the position and authority to document
them. The second, building security, important as it is, remains a bit of an illusion. The man with the gun was all too willing to kill anywhere he could.

But the main breakdown here is timing. These policies, helpful as they
are, are safeguards intended to keep already dangerous people from carrying
out the dangerous plots in their sick minds. And being so, they are doomed,
at least on occasion, to entirely fail.

Corporate America has sanctioned a certain amount of that failure, as it's
simply less expensive to pay off the damages after the bloodshed than to re-
visit the existing structures and policies with an eye toward preventing it in
the first place. God forbid it is your husband or wife, son or daughter,
mother or father, killed in that statistically acceptable occasion.

How brilliant it would have been, how noble, how wise and good, to
have studied in detail what led to that day in March, from every angle, from

the psychiatrist's office to the pharmacist's counter, to security practices and human resources policies, to unshakable union rules. To have tried to understand how a young man with such promise—promise my husband saw when he'd hired him nearly two years earlier—darkened within to such despair that bloodshed seemed his last and best resort. To have culled from that sad and difficult research the seeds of knowledge that might one day keep people from becoming violent in the first place.

But that would have required difficult and politically unpalatable work. The medical community would have had to admit that sometimes when they play God, they don't do it very well. The state bureaucracy in place for profitable decades would have had to open itself to genuine overhaul. A few people might have lost their jobs. The union wouldn't have stood for it.

And it was an election year.

Some months after that conversation with the acting president, early in the new year, I meet his wife at the grocery store. A talkative woman, sweetly uncomplicated and kind, her eyes are tired, the pretty features of her face are a little drawn, turning inward into an inadvertent frown. Dealing with a long illness, I'll learn. She leans away from me, just a bit distant, though despite the unpleasant exchange I'd had with her husband, one with which I am sure she is familiar—as I've heard through the corporation grapevine a number are—she's not at all unfriendly or unwilling to speak to me. Indeed, she wants to talk, wants me to know that after that conversation, her husband had tried. He had tried to speak with the director of security, to do as I had asked, tried to find out what went wrong that morning in March.

She wants me to know, standing there together, rows of canned goods behind us, that afterward he'd received a call from the governor's office, from the governor's chief of staff no less, instructing him to stop meddling. Telling him not to ask any more questions, telling him not to get involved, *if he knew what was good for him.*

That chief of staff has since been relieved of his duties. Resigned in disgrace, under investigation for assorted allegations of wrongdoing, among them pressuring the corporation into accepting contracts with cronies—the cleanup afterward awarded without bidding, expensive snow removal, and such. Worse as well.

The governor I so wanted to speak at Ott's funeral has resigned too, and been sent to prison.

You can read about it in the Hartford newspaper archives. It's all there in black-and-white. I couldn't dream up that sort of close-knit corruption if I tried.

Power corrupts, says my father, who at eighty retains a certain gut-founded admiration for guerrilla journalists and other sorts of bayonet-wielding freedom fighters, metaphoric or not, and fond remembrance for the passionate Communist friends of his youth. Through my own youth, through Watergate and Vietnam, LBJ's escalation of the bloodshed and Nixon's lies, horror stories unfolding on the nightly news or in depth on *Sixty Minutes*—which our family never missed, our ritual Sunday Mass of Enlightenment—my father would watch the screen in utter contempt, deriding the meritless rich and fatuous famous, the self-serving public officials in their shiny suits and capped teeth, yanking visionless on the reins of a wayward, bloated government. *Absolute power,* he continues, *corrupts absolutely.*

I don't know why, when the maxim I'd heard repeated two dozen times at the dining-room table of my adolescence morphed into the stuff of my own life, I was so surprised.

Would anyone believe, would anyone understand, if I were to say, if I could put it well into words, how keenly I recall him, how clear the memory remains, his fine form an arm's length away, his eyes dancing against the light, his voice and laughter ringing through the hall, how it remains, how it hasn't gone, these years, these years, as if he'd never left, as if I could still reach out and touch him, yes, that vivid, that true. What does that mean, what does that say, about my own mind, the savageness of it, to hold me in its own good time, a time that no longer is, and yet carries on, to send me such a vision in the early sun, in the warmth of my cheery north country kitchen, oven going, sweet cheesecake baking within, and there he is, there he is, standing just inside the doorway, then near the old oak table, an ancient burn-mark—an imperfect black heart—seared against the rich grain, he stands right there, as if to check the morning mail, and the breath goes out of me, the heart cannot take it all in without a pause. Who would believe, who would understand, who would not have me carted away for my own good and the good of the children, medicated into sensibility, talk-therapied into the concrete present, into the full weight of this world? No, you cannot possibly convey to another living being such a thing, the awful tricks with which your mind deceives you in the very light of day, and how grateful you are to have them play.

I mark in my mind the nine-month anniversary, falling just under three weeks until Christmas. We march out into the cool evening air, rope what's salvageable of the outdoor lights onto a bushy pine at the foot of the drive, or rather onto its bottom half, as we've no sturdy ladder and we're all too short to reach the top. Even so, it's a cheerful sight, that skimpy string glow-ing against the dark, and with it I unleash the demons of commercialization on the holiday season. *There will be a Christmas after all,* I vow, anticipating the morning runs to Toys "R" Us and Westfarms Mall, new ornaments for the tree and house, sweet old movies on the television, elementary school as-semblies where all the best politically correct seasonal songs will be sung. Whatever the tariff, whatever the toil, it doesn't matter. The kids will want for nothing this year.

A stranger sends me a check for my children, for me to buy them pre-sents, and I'm ashamed to say I cash and spend it greedily.

I imagine I spend plenty on myself as well that season, though just on what I can't recall.

Christ, the days just get better and better, I write in my journal. My PhD chapter boomerangs back in the mail to me, covered (at least for the first half, at which point we can assume the professor simply gave up), with pen-ciled comments and suggestions and a handful of question marks as well. At-tached is a letter, one I fail to keep for posterity; it soundly though not without its measure of kindness and diplomacy, kicks me out of the doctoral program. I recall in essence the professor writing, *Given the length of time away from study, the obvious difficulties in working independently and at a dis-tance on this project, I'll have to recommend to the director that you not continue at this time . . .*

I can't blame the woman, though I wanted to, though I felt then and do now that the work wasn't altogether that shabby. Still, I had to admit I was hardly PhD material, I never had been. I'd spent my graduate days focused on corralling Ott into matrimony and then setting up house, and had dis-tinguished myself not through Shakespearean scholarship or academic net-working savvy, but by parading about in the finest collection of high heels ever to see those hallways and getting myself pregnant with voluptuary ease and frequency.

"My, you're a fertile little thing!" the gorgeous blue-eyed professor of ro-manticism had said to me, passing in the hall, newly detected twins beneath the pleats of a rather pretty maternity dress. Another professor, on hearing the news, kissed me heartily on the cheek.

That more or less sums up my graduate school achievements and repute. My father-in-law, who enjoyed goading me into emotion-charged debate, would say to me as I swung open the door after an afternoon seminar or a morning of teaching, "So how's it going at the doorknob factory?" That irreverence for academia bristled with me, mostly because I secretly harbored a fair amount of it myself.

The rejection of the dissertation chapter is humiliating, of course. I'd told every human being who'd displayed the slightest interest that I was going back to school, I would finish the doctorate, I would take care of my family, thank you very much, I'd not be dependent on handouts, on a death benefit, on a pension from the state of Connecticut. I'd make my own money. I'd carve my own path.

And on the strength, or rather lack of it, of my *writing,* that vision collapsed. My writing. The only game I had going. I read the paper again, thinking, *If the complaints were on mechanics, structures, sources, I'd fix them, I'd ask for another chance.* But there's hardly a positive comment anywhere in the thirty-some pages. There's not a single toehold to keep from falling off the side of the cliff.

I relate this latest catastrophe to my therapist, tell him how friends I've confided in have been supportive, but still how embarrassed I am, ask him how I should respond to the professor. Should I send her a note and thank her for reading the chapter? Tell her I honestly thought I had written a decent paper, apologize for wasting her time?

We've come to know each other a bit over these months, the therapist and I, or rather he's come to know me, and I can sense he's peeved by this. He, too, had hoped for smoother sailing. He'd like a victory for me, something to simply go my way. He looks at me squarely and says, "You don't owe her anything. You don't have to write to her."

And so I don't.

Maybe she did me a favor, the beautiful Nabokov scholar. Maybe I would have been utterly miserable, found myself unable to keep up with studies and children both, lost the necessary interest and resolve along the way, flunked the grueling oral exams after years of writing and research. But it shook me, this failure. It knocked the wind out of my already shaky self-confidence, provided another lump of emotional coal in my holiday stocking. Another disappointment, another fixation to mourn and fear as I faced the turning of the calendar.

With each marking of another day, I'd hoped I'd do better, feel better. Be stronger, be smarter. But December was turning into one giant sinkhole.

Along with the holiday school concerts and the massive shopping trips to the mall and Toys "R" Us comes the difficult business of the year's end: the probate work still not complete, investments not yet in my name, death certificates and appropriate cover letters waiting to be forwarded to the proper authorities. March 6 is, according to Fox News, the second biggest story of 1998; I'll not remember the first. I see it all played out again on the television screen. Reminders abound. Sending out Christmas cards minus one name. Readying for the holidays alone.

Keeping my emotions in check, my voice regulated around the kids, is an awesome task. Frequently I fail, and the shame of failing haunts me. I turn inward. I want to hide. I seek out simple diversions, in flowers and soft music, in funny movies, in the sunshine beating through the glass in my greenery-filled Florida room. Anything to offset the mood of the long days, to soothe the pummeling of bad dreams: of Ott lying forever on the bed of stone, of someone stabbing me, leaving a deep incision in my side, like the Roman soldier who plunged a lance under Christ's left rib, to confirm his death on the cross.

Jesus died from suffocation, I write in my journal, *from exposure to the elements. He couldn't hold his body up to breathe.*

This comes in the entries just before Christmas, love letters addressed to a dead man.

After midnight Christmas Eve, I am still up wrapping the loot I'd hidden in closets and, when those were full, under a blanket along the wall beside my bed. They're hardly works of art, these two-dozen-or-so papered gifts, but they're covered and taped and tagged, and finally set out beneath the tall, full tree I've asked the husband of a friend to cart home for us. A stack of presents three feet tall, so many thousands of dollars worth of toys and electronics that saying the amount aloud today would make me shudder. But the kids must have their Christmas, nothing must be amiss in the early morning melee. I even photograph the scene before I go to bed, as if to document it, to prove to myself and others *Life goes on.*

And if I believed in ghosts, which of course I do, then I would say we are visited with one that night. Every floorboard in the house creaks under weightless footsteps, the door to the basement down the hall rattles against its ineffectual lock. Several times I am convinced we have an intruder in the house, and I get out of bed and turn on lights, check windows, the sliding glass doors. Nothing. And when I return to bed, the noises start again.

By quarter to five, the children are awake, calling out for me to get up with them, that Santa (*wink, wink*) has come and gone, and left a mountain behind. In no time they are gleefully scaling the rock face. I make coffee and watch the delightful turmoil, the insolent shredding of foil wrap, the manhandling of cardboard and foam to expose the treasures encased within.

My son, age ten, sets up his new computer and has it fully operational in just over an hour. Later, he will tell me, "Even though Dad isn't here, we're still having a good Christmas."

The day after, I decide to decimate the small and dreary master bath. I rip off chunks of stained wallpaper, unscrew ugly towel racks, dislodge an ancient medicine chest from its poorly positioned alcove. I don't know why I think this will make me feel any better. "Try not to knock down a load-bearing wall," a friend advises, hearing of the latest attempts to transform the house into something it no longer is. "Be a mite bit careful with that sledgehammer."

This is the fifth room since March to suffer my redecorating wrath. It'll be the last. Before I've even bagged and tossed the debris, I start surfing the Internet for real estate farther north.

And here, a tip for the lonely: Want to make a quick friend? Call a realtor.

The holidays come to an end, and none too soon. I've wished them away, telling myself, *Just get through it, just get through it.* The drying tree sheds its short, fragrant needles on the new blue carpet; we forget to switch on the strand of lights on the bare limbs at the end of the drive. Most of the toys have already become little more than irrelevant gadgets, taking up space, their bellies full of dead batteries. In New York City, the glowing ball has fallen once again, not that I bothered to witness it; the morning crowds have left the parade routes and settled into comfortable sofas strategically positioned three feet in front of televisions to watch the bowl games.

There's a half-bottle of Jack Daniels in the cabinet above the refrigerator. I take it down and pour some into a squat glass, straight, no ice, just the way the Good Lord intended. I bring it to my lips and take a sip. *Oh, yeah,* I think, raising the glass in salute to no one there. *Happy fucking New Year.*

I don't know how much I drink, maybe not a lot, I've lost the tolerance I once had, and mercifully, I remember little of the evening in that sodden spell. A long phone call to a girlhood friend in Delaware, another to the cousin who knows me well, during which my chatty mood takes a sudden dive and I reveal, with no small shame, "I hate my life." Stumbling in the kitchen, the sweet hard liquor coming up, back into the glass. The frightened kids helping me to the couch.

In the morning the girls will think, or I persuade myself they might, that I was sick, I had the flu. But my son knows better. "Did you mean that?" he asks, breaking my heart. "Did you mean you hate your life?"

"Of course I don't," I say, kissing his dark hair. "I wasn't myself last night."

When I tell my therapist at the next session, he hardly raises a brow. He knows what the holidays can bring, the emotional train wrecks of the happy season, he's seen it before. But I'm horrified at my behavior. I'm shaken at last quite soundly out of my coddled self-pity and vow my children will never see me that way again. And they never do.

I need to change everything, I write in my journal. *A new start away from all this heartache.* I must move on.

And, *God help me. Help me do the right thing.*

"We're moving," I tell them. "We're leaving Connecticut. I can't stand it here another minute."

It's a long weekend, the Martin Luther King, Jr., holiday, the weather is wretched, the drive once we hit Vermont nothing short of life-threatening. The left lane of Interstate 91 is unplowed, the right just a pair of icy furrows where other cars have traveled. We're on our way to Montpelier, to my brother's home, and then in the morning to North Hero, an island in Lake Champlain, to see an old farmhouse on six acres. It sounds like a dream, a piece of paradise somehow within budget. We follow the realtor's directions and meet her there, my brother driving us the many miles, civilization dwindling, buildings growing sparse. He's vetoed another house I'd hoped to see; he tells me the town is too remote and downtrodden, no place to raise young children. I've limited choices for this trip; this house had better do.

It's well kept, with a steep pitched roof and a large, obvious addition to the left, cheery enough from the outside, though set too close to a road that I am sure in the summer becomes a freeway. The realtor turns the key and in we go, to inspect what seems to me the handiwork of a number of owners, each stamping his unskilled thumbprint upon the place. The window in one bedroom is broken, and all the bedrooms are small, shoved up into what should be merely an attic for storage of a few boxes of knickknacks. The stairway rising to them has flimsy, mismatched rails.

From the porch I can see in the far distance the blue-gray mountains of New York across the broad expanse of ice and snow, which is the lake in deep winter. The whiteness goes on nearly forever, and I can't help but think what it might be like to be trapped in the middle of it, freezing to death over a long black night.

It's on the porch I start to cry. I can't control it; I let the tears fall while away from the others. Fooling no one, I tell the realtor, *We'll take it.* In her

Burlington office, after a sob-filled car ride, I make a low offer, hand her a deposit check for $5,000. It's a joyless thing, but it's done.

Late that evening she calls, tells me the owners have rejected the figure. She's not surprised when I don't counter.

There's one more house I decide we'll stop to see on our way home to Connecticut, though it's an hour and better out of our way, on the other side of the state in the rural Northeast Kingdom, and the next morning's weather is again frightening. An even older home, in need of no small repair, and at the very limit of my budget to boot. But we've come this far. We might as well.

The realtor, a tall, robust man nearing retirement age, clasps my hand, unlocks the heavy backdoor, tells me the house has been empty nearly three years. It's a great big cube, Georgian Colonial, circa 1798. The black shutters are askew, minus slats; they remind me of a mouth full of crooked and missing teeth. Inside it's just as cold as out, no heat, the pipes drained, the electricity off. As the sun is hiding behind ominous clouds, the house seems at first dreary despite the many twelve-over-twelve windows, the tasteful paper in every room. The floors and walls are dusty, the basement is low, settled, a little spooky. The ceilings bloom with muddy brown spatters and concentric rings like those inside an old tree, the telltale signs of ice dams, a leaky roof.

But it's inviting, the house, uncomplicated as an open palm. Immediately the kids are running about, examining the nearly perfect symmetry of its construction, the wide central staircase, the graceful, plentiful woodwork in the parlors, the deep red and gold toile paper in the chandeliered dining room. I hear shouts—"This room's mine!" "I get this one!"—and descending those stairs, I imagine myself, on cold winter mornings, tying my bathrobe tight around me as I walk down in the dark to start breakfast, to put on a pot of coffee to perk.

"I'm obliged to tell you that the house is haunted," the realtor says, reciting the story of Daniel Cahoon, the man who built the house with his son two centuries ago, who got drunk one afternoon and was gored to death, saving a grandchild from the wrath of a rampaging bull. He died in one of the upstairs bedrooms, and in her grief, his widow boarded up the wine cellar. People have been looking for that wine cellar ever since, he says. It's a documented fact.

He wants to know if it'll upset me, the ghost, if it will cost him a sale, this restless spirit whose boots have been heard pounding on the stairs for a couple hundred years now, who's said to be still looking for that wine cellar himself.

But I'm not afraid. What's one more ghost?

I've fallen in love with the old house nestled deep in the snow.

I never even look at the town, which, upon inspection a month later, turns out to be in bulk the intersection of two streets of shops, busy and well kept, two banks, two bookstores, a library, a Chinese restaurant, the post office, the corner grocery store. I don't drive up the dirt road that leads to the hilly woods beyond the house, don't question the rusting pipe jutting out of the snow which the realtor says is an old well to test the groundwater. I don't consider the neighborhood or the busy road, or the small car dealership two hundred yards beyond. I simply know this is my house. Back in Connecticut, after consulting with my father by phone on the risks and merits of buying a historic home, and weighing the veracity of the report that folks from California are ready to grab it up for use as a bed-and-breakfast, I call the realtor and offer top dollar.

The corporation, as a quasi-private concern, is regulated by the state of Connecticut; the board of directors, all appointed by the governor, has named a new president. It's not the acting president, not my husband's friend, but rather the man who oversaw that regulation. My husband didn't much enjoy regulation of any sort. His dealings with this man were, I expect, begrudgingly cordial. In those days, when Ott would return from work, pulling off his tie, replacing the polished dress shoes for comfortable Topsiders, telling me of the latest high-level bureaucratic tedium, I thought of those two men a little as bulls, lumbering around one another in a respectful if unresolved standoff. In their way, in their balance, with the perspective of time, I suppose together they made a good team.

Early in the year, this new president issues a statement. He declares that under the previous leadership the corporation had emphasized the wrong things. The implication being of course that under his leadership they'll emphasize what's right.

I take that implication poorly.

I know this man. He came to my house that day in March, told me what I already knew, but also of the others who had been killed. And he'd come once before for a holiday party, his pretty wife at his side.

I met him again, a few years ago. A scholarship had been created in my husband's name, and I flew to a conference in Nova Scotia to present the first award at a gala dinner. And the new president was there, in the audience. At a reception later, too nervous to eat, and the wine finally hitting me, I started to cry when a song reminded me too keenly of one who wasn't there. And the new president, who had just happened by, stayed with me the rest of the evening, listening to me go on. We took a walk by the water, and he held my hand. I was grateful for that.

Every sixth of the month since March, I mark the day, I remember that morning, I remember my husband. I'm troubled by the time that's passed. How can he be dead for nearly a year? What have I done with myself, what have I to show?

As the anniversary approaches, I ask myself how it ought to be observed, what is appropriate, what will have meaning, in light of all that's been left undone. What will the corporation do in remembrance? Little if anything, I imagine. Organize an interfaith service for the employees, to which the families will be invited as an afterthought, some sunny morning spiritual matinee where we'll all hold hands and sing Kumbaya. Reporters will be alerted, of course; they'll cover it from the back pews, write upbeat pieces about "moving on."

And that happened, of course. There was indeed such a service, to which I was invited, quite late. I did not attend. Can't tell you, then, if they actually sang.

Before the anniversary arrived, providence intervened, in the form of an invitation from an editor at the Hartford paper, responding to the latest letter of mine, a stream of eviscerating adjectives about the use of my husband's photo on their Web site. No, he says, he won't remove the photo. But he offers to meet, to talk, and I accept.

In my journal I write, *It's time I spoke out.*

And now, with this proposal, this open hand, I know how.

I make a call to that handsome sergeant who met me for coffee those months ago, who makes an inquiry of his own and gets back to me. "The case is closed," he says. "You can do whatever you like with the witness statements. If anyone asks, just say you received them through proper channels."

I don't consult with my attorney, I don't second-guess my gut instinct. I place the copy I've had made along with that red-bound police report inside a simple fake suede portfolio I've carted about since graduate school days, put on a dark suit, and drive to downtown Hartford. From the cheerless expanse of the lobby, I'm escorted to an upper-floor office, far away from the noise of the busy pressroom, a sanctuary crowded with weighty furniture.

The editor asks if I mind that he's invited a reporter to join us, the same reporter who interviewed my husband time and again about corporation business, who had written that in his last meeting with the man with the gun, the murderer-to-be had literally frothed at the mouth.

I don't mind.

They sit me at the head of the wide, imposing table, and take positions on either side. I fidget in the heavy seat fit for a king, nervously toy with the portfolio I can't seem to decide to either hold or set against the leg of the chair.

"I am here," I say at last, "because I am *disgruntled.*" I perch the case on my lap and open it. "You've seen this," I say, not quite a question, pulling out the papers bound in red. The reporter indicates that he has. I set it aside. "But you haven't seen this." I bring out the witness statements, the documents the attorneys themselves have yet to acquire, the secret file unavailable for review by any member of the press. I place the pile on the table's glossy surface.

If the men exchange glances, they're subtle, betraying nothing. They stay quiet, waiting for me, and I say, "I don't know if there's a story here. I'm too close to it, I can't be impartial." But I tell them that no internal investigation has taken place, no one's learned what ought to have been learned from this tragedy, because no one's asked the vital questions or faced what must be done. You can't prevent what happened from happening again, I say, without an accurate and honest assessment of what led up to it in the first place.

The mood is somber, the men largely silent. Through the tunnel of memory, the room is dark, though we sit beside a wall of tall windows. The sky is a yellow gray, as if penciled in on vellum. I can remember their eyes, the men. Shadowed, deep.

"So here it is," I say. "Here it is. I don't know what you'll think after reading the statements. You decide what there is to report."

"But someone," I say, "someone should tell the truth."

The editor helps me on with my coat. The reporter walks me to my car in the light rain. "He was always a gentleman," he says of my husband, of the manner in which he handled the frequently adversarial questions he was posed. He takes my hand and wishes me the best.

"Were they salivating?" the one friend in whom I confide later asks. "Do you have any idea what you handed them today?"

My lawyer and all the other March 6 lawyers have prepared papers to file, a notice of intent, an acknowledgment of our forthcoming suit. My neighbor, an attorney and good friend, serves as a conduit, my own attorney's office being many towns away. He brings over the fax, sits with me at the dining-room table, turns the pages in his hands as he reviews what it all means, what's about to be set into motion.

From the legalese the bare facts emerge, the black-and-white, the bold outlines of what took place that Friday morning, the picture I've allowed time to blur: How he was shot, by whom, and when. Where the bullets traveled, and where he fell. What wasn't done to save him, what might have been.

"You have to give the go-ahead," my neighbor says. "You need to call the office and tell them to proceed."

After he leaves, I pick up the phone, unable to put the papers aside, reading them through teary, stinging eyes. The paralegal's voice is deep and soothing; her tone unhurried. I imagine her on the other end, checking off something in a box, or writing a simple note to herself.

"File the papers," I say. "Yes. File. Do everything you can."

He was always a gentleman, the reporter had said, and yes, he was, and yes, I remember, I have not forgotten the man who was lost, and why this matters, why I can't be silent any longer.

I think about his last words. I think about our children, how his greatest fear was that something would happen to them. Now and then his dreams would be haunted with imagined injuries, kidnappings, car crashes in which not everyone survived.

Someday, when they are ready, when they decide to look back, they'll ask to see the news reports I've set aside, the hundreds of yellowing cards and letters of condolence, the clippings about his distinguished career. They'll review these things with the eyes of young adults, they'll see the gentleman, the hero, the entrepreneur, they'll see a side of him largely unknown at the edge of a soccer field, unspoken over a box of doughnuts and glasses of milk on a Saturday morning.

And then they'll turn to me with a single question. I foresee it, I can feel it, it's what I would wonder, what I'd want to know as well. "What did *you* do, Mom," they'll ask, "after he was killed?" I can hear it now, the injustice in their voices, in their only appropriate inquiries; I can sense their impatience with a casual response. "What did you do to right the wrong?"

I want to be able to look straight into their eyes, to tell them without qualification or doubt, *I did everything I could.*

I've asked, and the reporter and editor have agreed, that my name not appear in whatever might come of our meeting. I want to write a piece of my own, an editorial, to tell of how I failed to make a difference, but that I had tried. I speak several times with the op-ed editor, who is gracious and kind, who tells me he welcomes my submission, though I suspect, given the timing, the approach of the anniversary, and the bounty of those witness statements I handed over, the paper would publish anything I'd give them— a grocery list, a haiku suitable for a greeting card. But I'm grateful for the podium, if a little nervous. A sensitive friend, my "big sister," tells me wisely to be careful, she feels negative energy around me, people ready to exploit the situation. She doesn't trust the corporation, or those at the paper, for that matter; she warns me to rely on no one. My father cautions me on the phone, he fears reprisals and ill will. I fear simply the news stories won't go deep enough.

I've played the hand that was dealt me, and there's nothing left to do but wait for the dealer to draw. I turn my mind elsewhere, imagine the roses and geraniums I'll grow when I move into my new home. I buy luxurious cosmetics imported from Italy. I let myself believe that I will love again, and be loved in return.

And in my mind, I write a letter to the mother of the man with the gun. I think of her, how she has suffered too, think of how I might ask if we could pray for peace together, for God's healing for everyone.

But I am sure such a letter would sound pompous, or self-serving, or insincere. And I tell myself that I can't know the mind of the woman who raised the man with the gun. She might very well blame me, blame my family, for the sadness that together, separately, we have lived. She might tear into tiny pieces anything I would send, cursing in spirit the man her son had cursed in the flesh, to his face, in their dying, savage moments.

I'm working on that piece for the paper, the editorial in which I will relate a bit of the sad history of letters I have uselessly composed and sent, of the ineffectual appearance before the board, of the fruitless search for answers. I imply, of course, I need to have it understood, that I've done my best. I say outright how I long for normalcy, for life again, for "laughter and music."

And while I'm reviewing those words, perched on the old foldout sofa bed in the falling light of a late afternoon, that silly Wal-Mart commercial comes on the television, the one with the bouncing yellow happy face, the snapping whip and the Western tune. *Rollin', rollin', rollin'* . . . And I remember how I used to turn that song on its head for a little amusement, twisting it into a play on the governor's name, changing the lyrics to fit the latest Connecticut crisis, a feeble joke for sure, but a running one my husband and I shared. How it made him grin. How he enjoyed my cynicism.

And it's enough, the cheerful memory coming back to me, the coincidence of song and smile, enough to draw me away from the fire for a little cool air. And I laugh, going with it, laugh right out loud, singing it again for no one to hear, letting the notes trip like tart candy off my tongue.

That cold February carries on, each gray afternoon a small mountain to climb. An aged uncle in the Midwest suffers a stroke, the battery in the Volvo dies three times. I read books with titles like *To Begin Again,* I unclog the shower drain, I pretend that the $50 jar of volcanic mud from Sicily will make me look five years younger. I fight off a cold, and rejoice at the higher grades on my son's latest report card and make plans for my daughters' birthday.

But nothing matters more than the mere passing of time. I want these weeks done and gone; I want this year of mourning to come to an end I can somehow tolerate. We'll squirm through a memorial Mass for Ott and an uncomfortable gathering at the house afterward, but it's the story in the paper that will soundly mark the year. I'm like a pagan at Stonehenge, waiting for the sun to rise through the tunnel of rock, heralding the longed-for lengthening of the days.

Months earlier, in a self-pitying funk, I had discontinued delivery of the newspaper, tired of corporation stories, tired of Connecticut. The reporter with whom I'd met in that soundproof boardroom alerts me: be sure to read the Sunday paper. The one friend in whom I confide fights the new snow and brings me a copy, and together we sit at the dining-room table, the gaudy brass chandelier above us shining like Christmas in the dim morning light.

There's not one story; there are three, all on the front page. The bold headline reads, "Was It Avoidable?" My friend and I read the articles together, pointing out passages to one another, stunned with what's revealed, somber yet pleased with the reporter's excellent work on the lead. We conclude that anyone with a conscience would have answered the headline, "Yes."

Because this is what the reporter did: he read those statements, of course, he studied them, it's clear. And then he met with corporation executives, with the president, with the head of human resources, with the chief of security. They met with him gladly, we can assume, eager perhaps to share the progress they had made in the difficult year, the gratifying transition to new quarters, to new leadership, the rejuvenation of employee morale.

Only, the reporter charted an unexpected course. He led them back to that Friday morning in March, to a place they'd not wanted to go. The chief of security, the head of human resources, wouldn't have known that the reporter had seen those buried statements. They'd have no reason to believe the line they'd delivered all those months ago would soundly trip them up, as he exposed the discrepancies between public accounts and those given to the police immediately after the murders, when the blood was being cleaned from the walls and sprayed away from the gray bed of stone. When perhaps truth meant something more dear than pride or position.

What did my husband know of the employee who would become the man with the gun? I can only tell you what I know myself, what he said to me, in the one conversation I recall. That in late summer or early fall of 1997, he believed he could no longer be trusted to perform his job, that one of the men he would later kill worried he would compromise the computer system. His behavior had become erratic; he was upset over a long-standing grievance and a failed office romance. He'd shaved his head, he'd traded shoptalk with the head of security about guns. He was a possible threat. And despite being told the union wouldn't stand for it, that the corporation would be sued, my husband wanted him fired, out, gone.

And then, suddenly, quickly, before I had time to dwell on the matter, thank God, he was gone. Out on extended medical leave, good riddance, gone gone gone, under the care of a psychiatrist, getting the help he obviously needed.

I never thought about that employee again until that morning in March. My husband said nothing of his return to the workplace earlier that week. But when that pretty blonde reporter announced there'd been a shooting at the corporation, I knew immediately who had aimed the gun, and I knew my husband was dead.

So when you read in that article the assertions of those who survived, that no one had concerns about this man, that the act was merely routine when the chief of security, who was not permitted to carry a gun, brought his own firearm to work in October 1997, or when the head of human resources declares that no one wanted the man with the gun fired, that all was employee-relations peaches and sweetened cream, when she denies that she herself was worried, though she refused to meet with him alone—understand, then, the year of lies they told themselves and others, the blockade they erected to protect the corporation from liability, the depth of their dishonor to the dead.

Why did he come back to work, then, if he was still so unstable, why did the psychiatrist approve that return, despite the hostility he'd voiced in their sessions, the vengeful comments, the suicidal thoughts he had expressed?

His medical leave was about to run out. The man with the gun had received a letter to that effect. God knows the amount of paperwork an extension might have required.

At that uncomfortable gathering after the memorial Mass, I'm standing in the dining room with a business associate of my husband's, a decent man, intelligent, kind. Charming, even. He's quizzing me about the great old house I've bought, buoying me gently along the uneasy flow of conversation. Then he asks if I've seen the newspaper.

I tell him I think it's the best article I've ever read in my life.

We are inches away from one another, nibbling good food my friends have brought to the house, to make the day easier for me. And he says, "Wow. You still are angry."

I can think of nothing to say to him.

There will be, in the months to come, none of the reprisals my father fears, no openly expressed ill will. No elucidating statements from the corporation, no policy changes, no reworking of a fatally flawed bureaucracy.

But, then, that's not my fault.

Have you forgiven the man with the gun? the moderator at a conference at which I'm invited to speak wants to know. He asks us all, we're all survivors, one atrocity worse than the next, sitting on the stage beneath the bright lights, passing the microphone from one to another.

Five years have gone by. I think I know what the answer ought to be, as a woman who finally wants to live, who wants to be fully human. But I've not yet come to that place of relative peace.

The best I can do is not think about him at all, I say. *I'm not sure forgiveness for such an act is mine to give.*

With the appearance of those news articles, I feel no need to publish anything myself. The reporter and his colleagues have brought a clarity to the subject I could not have achieved. Anything I might add at this point has been rendered simply personal and largely irrelevant, a grieving woman's belated rant. But I've made a promise, and the paper wants to use the piece, as the cover for their Commentary section, the editor says, that first Sunday in March.

On that morning I rise early. I'm poking about the house before the kids awake, turning up the heat, perking coffee. I pass by the picture window in the dining room and see a tall man all in gray standing in the driveway. He's walking toward the end, as if to retrieve the newspaper, even though it's not there, the issue with my article inside.

When I get closer to the window, the man is suddenly gone. There are no footprints in the fresh blanket of snow.

7

We the Living

BEFORE WE LEAVE FOR VERMONT, GOOD NEIGHBORS TAKE US TO BRUNCH. They have gifts for the children, and one for me, a wire-bound journal decorated with a flower painted in watercolor purple and pinks, and these words in square calligraphy: "And then the day came when the risk to remain tight in a bud was more painful than the risk it took to blossom." A quote from Anaïs Nin, my girlhood idol, whose many volumes of journals I read and absorbed through the skin.

It broke my heart, later on, when I learned a fair number of those vivid entries had been fabricated or enhanced, a pretty lie added here and there to belie boredom, make the commonplace seem less so, or to bolster a booming ego. Discovering that as a grown woman she'd slept with her father, and rather creatively at that, didn't help much either. But she led a passionate, unusual life, Anaïs Nin, rich in relationships with interesting people, among them a number of famous men. She had two husbands, the second a far younger man. She didn't bother to divorce the first. She danced the tango and wore extraordinary costumes and painted each room in her house in Louveciennes a different vibrant color. She threw marvelous dinner parties that lasted long into the night, no one wanting to leave her table.

And the woman could write.

I understand, of course, the desire to embellish, to beautify, to turn the mundane to music, and the ease with which a woman who loves words, who plays language as a game, can rearrange the drearier stuff of her life into a story more beguiling on the page than it unfolded in the punishing light of day. But it's a treacherous skill, fine for crafting fairy tales and fiction, poisonous when the subject is your own self. At that, it ought to be squelched at every turn.

117

I'd put the Connecticut house on the market in March, at too low a price, and after an expensive professional cleaning and a single showing, it sells in two days to a thirty-something couple with infant twins. The couple immediately insist that close to a dozen items be repaired or replaced or credited toward the purchase. My realtor, a woman who came highly recommended, lays open my checkbook at their disposal. They want windows fixed, the roof mended, the septic system dug anew. A pipe in the basement seems to be leaking; the plumber called in reports it's nothing but condensation. Then there's a panic over termites, and another expert at owner expense inspects the premises to relieve the buyers' fears, and sprays the foundation with pesticide in an act he himself says is completely unnecessary. After six weeks or so of this, at the pre-closing inspection, the buyers will complain that the fireplace has not been adequately emptied of ash. This will cost me $75.

I've had it with them.

The old washer and dryer in the little room leading to the garage have seen better days. There are tricks to dealing with these demented appliances, tricks I've learned and would have happily shared with anyone not so obviously out to gouge me. And yet, capable as I am to provide a bit of comfort and support to the buyers, I do not confide. I keep this small wisdom to myself. I neglect to inform the pair that one valve on the washer is a little temperamental, that the pressure must be modulated in a particular way to prevent, oh, say, a tidal flood on the floor. Nor do I relate that the dryer door requires gingerly handling, that it must be pulled out slightly askew or it will jam open like a gaping mouth, blocking the exit to the garage, and for perhaps the better part of an afternoon one might be stuck trying to ease the ragged hinges back into their misaligned grooves.

But they were a smart young couple, quick studies both. I suspect they discovered these tricks all on their own.

We hire tall, strong men to pack and cart our houseful of belongings north. An expensive indulgence, but one I do not regret. It would cost $600, however, to dismantle and move my husband's pool table, which has remained largely unused all these months. I sell it, at a good price. But it's a stupid mistake. I miss it now.

As we begin to settle into our new home, the dozens of boxes parceled out, stacked along walls, interrupting the flow of traffic in the kitchen, the heavy furnishings placed just where I asked, and clean linens finally on the beds, I see my son walking about the hallways. He's taking into every room a framed photo of his father, one of my favorites, a studio shot from our

Delaware days, his smile uncomplicated, his eyes that melting chocolate brown. My son's dark eyes.

And he tells me, when they've completed their inspection, turning to me with an insider's grin, "Dad says we got a good deal!"

The front-page headline of the local paper reads, just days after we arrive, "Puppies Abandoned in St. Johnsbury."

In no time flat, the lovely bubble of my new paradise breaks. The town we've relocated to is tiny indeed, without any of the amenities to which the kids feel entitled—no Blockbuster or Bertucci's, no Gap, no glittery two-story mall. And the house, gorgeous as it is, as deeply as I love it already, is two centuries of trouble in the making. The week we move in, the upstairs toilet leaks, ruining the kitchen ceiling below. The bathrooms are anti-quated, the porcelain pitted, the plumbing in two of the three continually untrustworthy. The side door that has been boarded up for years to keep out the cold and block a broken fanlight will take serious money to restore. The three-dozen windows are drafty and tricky to handle; I open one and it falls completely out of its frame. In a fit of remodeling zeal, I run over the power cord while working a hand sander on a painted floor and nearly electrocute myself.

I need a live-in Bob Vila.

My son reports that on the bus ride to school that very first morning, the other kids ask if he's a vampire or a werewolf; since he lives in the haunted house, he must be a freak. My daughters miss their Connecticut playmates.

Dear God, what have I done?

No, no time for regrets. We're on an adventure, we're pioneers. The girls and I explore our new terrain, discovering a funky bookstore and café in the neighboring town, a place to combine two of our favorite pastimes, eating and reading. Later another important find: a shop just a few miles south of the Canadian border, where all the most desirable Beanie Babies are for sale on its crowded glass shelves. And in no time at all, my son has a girlfriend. There's hope in the heart of each of us.

One day that April, two students in Littleton, Colorado, bring guns and bombs to their school and create the bloody havoc that forevermore one word will evoke: Columbine. Every morning after, I put the kids on the bus and worry anew.

In the years that follow, more fear and bloodshed: September 11, Afghan-istan, the ousting of Saddam. The guerrilla warfare afterward leaving so many dead, the continuing bloodshed across the holiest acres on earth, nuclear threat in the Far East.

I watch and read what's necessary of the news, enough to stay current and occasionally share an informed opinion. My love affair with *Sixty Minutes* is currently on hold.

I'm lucky enough to be hired part-time to teach freshman composition at the small state college set picturesquely in the hills just a few miles from my home. It's hard work for me—I'm not a natural teacher, I'm terribly nervous in front of people, and the only way I can get through it is to microchoreo-graph every class, to navigate from carefully constructed lesson plans: *Go to the board and pick up the chalk. Write your name, the course number, and the meeting time . . .* But it has its rewards, the students for whom you know you've made that proverbial difference, the one who wouldn't have passed without your extra help, the good word you put in at the departmental meeting on the exit exams, the several who leave cards and books in your office mail, sweetly expressing their thanks. Will I ever forget the brilliant, troubled kid who wrote an essay naming a certain type of bass guitar as the most significant achievement of the twentieth century? There are, of course, the teary moments, the stumbles over grammar I ought to know by heart, and those career-path questioning hours when, taking over a rowdy class from my expectant boss, I'm sure my time might be better spent raising goats in the backyard.

One semester I agree to teach a night course, a once-a-week slot I thought would be ideal. The students are a happy mix; many commuters traveling long miles, several kids with promise that shows in the first min-utes. A woman of my own age, returning to school, her husband having just survived a heart attack. She wants to be a nurse.

To my left sits a kid dressed all in black. His shirt reads, *Ask me how it feels to be a freak.* His nails are painted black, too, and I recall he's pierced here and there. He says nothing until I ask, as I do of every student, going around the room, what they fear most about writing.

He begins sensibly enough. But he goes on at length, gaining momen-tum, gathering an ominous steam, until he looks straight at me and says, "Writing is death."

I stand there, empty, dumb. Frightened. In a beat, a great kid across the room breaks the silence and says, "I was just worried about grammar!"

The tension is relieved, the students relax. And I carry on for the rest of the evening, jittery, though well enough, I suppose. But at home that night, and during the following days, I can't get the student out of my mind, his dress, his hostile stare, the danger I felt he could have become. He's been "red-flagged," I learn, he's an "exhibitionist," and I'm sure he's a problem waiting to happen. His manipulation of the class slaps me back to March 6, to the man with the gun, how easily one young man could be the other, and for the better part of a week, I find it hard to keep from crying, from remembering, not images of years ago, but the fear itself, the uncontainable fear. I try to contact my therapist in Connecticut, but he's moved on; we leave messages for one another, never do connect.

The student upsets me so that I call my boss and ask to have the class reassigned. It goes over poorly with the dean, I understand, and afterward I'm deeply embarrassed, my fledgling vocation in adjunct teaching certainly at stake. It won't be the last time I wish my weaknesses were easier to hide.

You see a young man like that, the darkness around him, the absence of hope, you wonder what on this good earth turned him so bitter, what love was lacking, what savage chemistry in the brain rages on. You thank God your own children have been spared.

They've grown, of course, my children, as children are wont to do, healthy and strong and optimistic in spite of it all. My girls are young women now; I'm told they look a little like me, but with softer features and sweeter smiles, their father's dark eyes, with his drive and athleticism. They are high achievers in the classroom, acknowledged stars on the soccer and track fields. My firstborn girl plays a wicked saxophone. She wants to be a famous actress, or write books, or save the rain forest; she has a near-fanatic intolerance of injustice and an uninhibited instinct to question authority, including mine. She organized a schoolwide protest to fight dress-code absurdities, and won. Her sister aims high, now toward law school; she pushes herself to succeed through honors classes and late night studying. An impeccable dresser, she has an eye for shade and form so refined she could consult to major fashion houses. And she goes for the jugular on the basketball court.

They are independent thinkers, loyal friends, competitive sisters, and loving daughters. I know how lucky I am.

My son is a young adult; he doesn't believe in regret, or in God. He never worries, because he knows I worry enough for him and the rest of the family as well. Throughout high school he attended to his studies on a "survival only" basis; he survived just fine. Now in college, studying computer programming, a gifted artist who dresses the part, he's added tones of gray and the occasional bloodred to balance the black. He loves dark, role-playing games and tall shapely blondes. Shapely blondes—and one in particular—love him in return. He has *me*, I am told, wrapped around his little finger.

All three of my children have rendered cynicism and the snappy come-back into nothing short of art forms. Being teenagers, they have acquired an enlightenment and knowledge of the world surpassed only by Siddhartha.

I spend altogether too much time thinking about the lives they will lead, wondering where they will build their homes, if they'll make good and happy choices in work and love. If they'll be blessed with children of their own.

And what do they remember of their father? What, after all these years, remains? Do the things I hang on to help, the images on the walls, the photos of him with Johnny Unitas and Steven Spielberg, the *New York Times* interview I framed that last Christmas, his Greg Norman bush hat I keep in the north parlor, his golf clubs sitting in the closet, his leather jacket I allow his son to wear, now and then, in clear, crisp weather?

When we talk of him, it's of good times, of Saturday mornings they spent with him one-on-one, of his favorite foods—fried okra and the smothered pork chops his mother taught me to prepare—his love of sports involving speed and endurance, and games of logic and skill. We talk of the pride he'd have in their latest accomplishments, of my son behind the wheel of his own red sports car, of the girls' consistent high honors and winning seasons. And I tell them, foolish as I am, that I believe from somewhere, some part of him sees them still, some energy and ties remain strong.

"Do you remember that moon?" one girl asks as we're driving home, looking through the windshield to see the full moon huge and heavy as a melon in the sky. "We saw a moon just like this one, when we were in Con-necticut." We'd been out for the evening, her father was driving. She'd wrig-gled up against the front seat to get a better view. And she remembers, and so do I, the simple cheerfulness inside the car that night, the contentment of being together, the warmth she found in the light of the full moon.

That first spring in the new house, I plant seven rose bushes beneath the kitchen window, a crowded fragrant row, a small orchard of fruit trees along the roadside, a little plot of tomatoes and herbs. The only room in the house that needs immediate cosmetic attention is the kitchen, which to me seems very sad. The countertop is fake marble laminate, and there's not enough of it; the flooring is worn brown linoleum; the cabinets of unadorned pine and wrought iron remind me of cheap caskets. I have only enough money to fix one thing on this list, so I choose the countertop, which I replace with flecked blue Corian, in a shade of the deep, dark sea, and add a movable island for more room to chop and knead.

The morning the work is completed, I am happily fussing about in my spiffed-up kitchen, running a damp cloth over the new countertops. Out of the corner of my eye, I see a woman draped in black float by the doorway. I see her, clearly, she's taller than I am, slender, her long arms covered in what might be lace. And this thought comes to me immediately, comes quickly to my mind: "There's the widow of the house," I conclude, "checking on the *new* widow of the house." I step out into the hall. The figure in black is gone.

Years later, though, I see her again, when I finally replace the aging floor. She comes back to investigate this latest improvement, and to see the new shelves across the picture window that hold a half-dozen African violets growing in antique teacups. She strides again across the kitchen doorway, only this time she is luminous, dressed head-to-toe in glowing white.

My father sees this as a good sign, a wedding perhaps. I think, simply, better times ahead. Maybe, peace of mind.

I've heard of women one hundred pounds, puny women like myself, hoisting the front ends of cars high in the air because someone they loved more than life itself was trapped beneath. Of mothers a thousand miles away knowing a child is in trouble, of men who could only be called angels pulling trapped motorists out of snowbanks, then disappearing without a trace.

I sensed something myself that morning in March, before I knew, before I saw the television screen. Still sitting at the computer, thinking suddenly I should get off the line, he might be trying to call. Feeling for a moment he was just over my left shoulder, signaling for my attention. A feeling I ignored.

We hear such stories. Sometimes, we live them. We wonder, we shrug, we smirk. We call it coincidence, or adrenaline rushing through the veins, anxiety misconstrued in hindsight as premonition, inner strength unknown until truly tested. We have our manageable theories.

But what if something deeper is at work, something beyond the comprehension of our imperfect senses, the narrow scope of sight and sound and smell, of touch and taste? What if a great sadness, a great shock, a great love or loss, changes the very fabric of our reality, breaks down if even for a moment in time the barrier between one world and the next, or of perhaps those existing side by side?

Is a woman who sees the dead in driveways or floating along the halls of her home taking measure of a world grown suddenly large, or is she simply mad?

I dream of my husband still, vivid dreams, though less frequent, and rarely of him lying on the bed of stone.

Sometimes he's angry, distant, his eyes focused far from my gaze. Sometimes he's standing beside me, smiling broadly, his arm cradling the small of my back.

Sometimes he's calling to me, and holding open a door.

Afterword

At the time of the Connecticut Lottery shootings, Ott Brown had spent more than a decade in the gaming industry, starting with his appointment as director of the Delaware Lottery. In 1993, he took over as president of the Connecticut Lottery, where he was instrumental in transforming the state agency into a successful quasi-public corporation. His background in business brought a unique dimension to state government; many throughout the lottery industry sought his advice and expertise.

The three other executives who lost their lives on March 6, 1998, were Linda Mlynarczyk, Michael Logan, and Frederick Rubelmann. Each was an admired, well-liked, and highly-skilled professional. Each was married. Linda, a certified public accountant, had served as mayor of New Britain, where her family had lived for four generations. Mike was a computer whiz, dedicated to both his work and family. He was only 33. Rick coached youth baseball, and was active in his community and at Saint Thomas Roman Catholic Church. Mike and Rick were both fathers of two.

According to newspaper reports, Mathew Beck, the young man who committed the killings, was taking night classes in computers. He was a New England Patriot fan and a devoted son to his father and mother. He was being treated for anxiety and depression, and had been prescribed medications which in some patients provoke hallucinations and outbursts of anger.